VIETNAMESE RECIPES

Genuine Vietnamese Recipes for the Entire Family

(Keep Calm and Try Vietnamese Cookbook)

Tracy Bryd

Published by Alex Howard

© **Tracy Bryd**

All Rights Reserved

Vietnamese Recipes: Genuine Vietnamese Recipes for the Entire Family (Keep Calm and Try Vietnamese Cookbook)

ISBN 978-1-990169-40-3

All rights reserved. No part of this guide may be reproduced in any form without permission in writing from the publisher except in the case of brief quotations embodied in critical articles or reviews.

Legal & Disclaimer

The information contained in this book is not designed to replace or take the place of any form of medicine or professional medical advice. The information in this book has been provided for educational and entertainment purposes only.

The information contained in this book has been compiled from sources deemed reliable, and it is accurate to the best of the Author's knowledge; however, the Author cannot guarantee its accuracy and validity and cannot be held liable for any errors or omissions. Changes are periodically made to this book. You must consult your doctor or get professional medical advice before using any of the suggested remedies, techniques, or information in this book.

Table of contents

PART 1 1

INTRODUCTION 2

DISHES NO. 1: CHICKEN WINGS FRIED FISH SAUCE "DROWNING" FAMILY MEAL 3
DISHES NO. 2: HOW TO COOK KOREAN HOT KIMCHI DELICIOUS 5
DISHES NO. 3: PESTO FRIED SHRIMP WITH GARLIC AND NUTRITIOUS POTATOES 7
DISHES NO. 4: THE RECIPE OF SHRIMP SAUCE WITH AN IRRESISTIBLE CREAMY AROMA 9
DISHES NO. 5: QUAIL EGGS FRY ME SNACKS EXTREME FUN MOUTH 11
DISHES NO. 6: STIR-FRIED SQUID WITH RICH COMPOTE SAUCE 13
DISHES NO. 7: STIR-FRIED SEAFOOD WITH CUCUMBER AND COOL MEDIUM 16
DISHES NO. 8: THE EGGS ARE JUST BOLD AND DELICIOUS IDEAL 18
DISHES NO. 9: STEAMED NOODLE SOUP NO ONE IS IRRESISTIBLE 20
DISHES NO. 10: PORK AND COCONUT EGGS MELT IN THE MOUTH 22
DISHES NO. 11: ROLLS OF VEGETABLES WITH A DELICIOUS AND BREATHTAKING 25
DISHES NO. 12: RE-LEMON BEEF SALAD 27
DISHES NO. 13: STIR FRIED SHRIMP WITH LOW-CALORIE ASPARAGUS, JUST KEEP THE SHAPE PERFECT 29
DISHES NO. 14: STIR FRIED SHRIMP WITH LEMON GARLIC 31
DISHES NO. 15: GARLIC PASTA SPAGHETTI 33
DISHES NO. 16: VEGETARIAN RICE RECIPE WITH RICH AND NUTRITIOUS VEGETABLES 35
DISHES NO. 17: FULL SWEET AND SOUR VEGETARIAN NOODLE 37
DISHES NO. 18: AROMATIC CHICKEN SOUP FOR WINTER TONIC 39
DISHES NO. 19: SALAD THAI CHICKEN CARROTS ARE PROTEIN AND GOOD FOR HEALTH ... 41
DISHES NO. 20: COOK DELICIOUS EEL VERMICELLI IS NO LESS THAN A RESTAURANT 44
DISHES NO. 21: NIKUJAGA - BEEF STEW WITH JAPANESE POTATOES 47
DISHES NO. 22: CHARMING, ATTRACTIVE WITH THE WELL-DICED BEEF 49
DISHES NO. 23: CRAB VERMICELLI BECOMES VERY EASY TO MAKE WITH THIS RECIPE 51
DISHES NO. 24: GO TO THE KITCHEN TO MAKE A DELICIOUS NUTRITIOUS LOTUS SEED CHICKEN SOUP 54
DISHES NO. 25: HOW TO COOK DELICIOUS THAI HOT POT SIMPLY AT HOME 56
DISHES NO. 26: REVEALING HOW TO MAKE DELICIOUS RIBS THAT CANNOT BE DENIED ... 59
DISHES NO. 27: ALL-WEEKEND BEEF NOODLES 61
DISHES NO. 28: RECIPE OF PORK INTESTINE STUFFED WITH MEAT THEN FRIED 63

DISHES NO. 29: GRILLED CHICKEN WITH A TASTY HONEY SAUCE, EAT THE RICE 65
DISHES NO. 30: HOW TO MAKE BEEF WITH TASTY TAMARIND SAUCE AS A RESTAURANT 67
1. BUN CHA (GRILLED PORK WITH RICE VERMICELLI NOODLE IN DIPPING SAUCE) 69
CHAR AND SLIGHTLY BOIL BEEF BONES 75
3. BANH DA CUA (RED NOODLE SOUP WITH CRAB) 78
4. NEM RAN (VIETNAMESE FRIED SPRING ROLLS) 82
WRAP AND FRY THE ROLLS 84
5. "NEM THINH" (PIG EARS AND MEAT COATED WITH POWDERED GRILL RICE) 86
6. SUA DAU NANH (SOY MILK) 89
7. BANH XEO MIEN TAY (VIETNAMESE SIZZLING CREPE) 92
8. XOI VO (SWEET RICE COATED WITH MUNG BEANS) 95
9. CHA CA LA VONG (LA VONG GRILLED TURMERIC FISH WITH DILL) 97
10.   GOI CUON (VIETNAMESE FRESH SUMMER ROLLS) 100

PART 2 103

RECIPES DIFFERENT TYPES OF VIETNAMESE DIPPING SAUCES 104

BASIC RECIPES 104
VIET-STYLE STOCKS 104
VEGETARIAN STOCK 106
ANNATTO OIL 106
PICKLED KOHLRABI AND CARROT 107
PICKLED CARROT AND DAIKON RADISH 107

DIPPING SAUCES (MOST POPULAR) 109

DIPPING SAUCE FOR BARBECUE MEAT 109
DIPPING SAUCE FOR SPRING ROLLS OR FRIED FOODS 110
DIPPING SAUCE FOR SEAFOOD 111
DIPPING SAUCE FOR SUMMER ROLL 112
PEANUT+HOISIN SAUCE 113
ANCHOVY SAUCE 113
TAMARIND FISH SAUCE 115
DIPPING SAUCE FOR DUMPLINGS 116
DIPPING SAUCE FOR STEAMED ROLLED RICE PANCAKE 116
DIPPING SAUCE FOR PANCAKO 118
VEGETABLES DIPS 118
VEGETARIAN DIPPING SAUCE 120

NOODLES & GLASS NOODLES ... 120

- Bún/Phở/Miến ... 120
- Beef Noodles Soup ... 122
- Beef Noodle Soup ... 125
- Beef Noodle Stir-Fry ... 125
- Grilled Pork Noodles ... 126
- Mixed Pho Noodles ... 129
- 'Thang' Noodle Soup ... 131
- Stir-Fry Glass Noodles With Crab Meat ... 135
- Hue-Style Beef Vermicelli Noodles Soup ... 138
- Vermicelli Noodles With Tilapia ... 141
- Vermicelli Noodles With Stir-Fry Beef ... 144
- Spring Roll ... 146
- Summer Rolls ... 150
- Beef Wrapped In Betel Leaves ... 154

RICE DISHES ... 157

- A Street Rice Stall In Hochiminh City ... 158
- Honey Lime Fried Chicken ... 158
- Caramelized Pork & Egg ... 160
- Caramelized Fish In Clay Pot ... 163
- Steamed Fish With Dill ... 166
- Braised Chicken With Shiitake Mushroom ... 167
- Salty And Spicy Grilled Chicken Wings ... 170
- Mocked Dog Meat ... 172
- Jellied Pork ... 174
- Shrimp Roasted With Salt ... 176
- Fried Eggs With Pork ... 179

CAKES ... 181

- Popular Street Food Cakes In Vietnam ... 181
- Steamed Rice Rolled Crepes ... 181
- Fried Rice Balls ... 185
- Crispy Fried Pancake ... 188
- Pillow Shaped Fried Dumpling ... **Error! Bookmark not defined.**
- Sweet Potato And Shrimp Cake ... **Error! Bookmark not defined.**

TAPIOCA DUMPLINGS .... **ERROR! BOOKMARK NOT DEFINED.**

Part 1

Introduction

For Vietnamese people, meals are not just full. Meals are also an opportunity to gather among family members or to meet friends and colleagues in an intimate, cozy atmosphere. In recent years, not only in Vietnam, but in many parts of the world, the focus has been on family meals more, because eating not only gives us health but enjoying food is also fun. Cooking is not only a job but also a hobby. In Vietnamese kitchens, many kinds of spices, pickles, melons, eggs, as well as dried fish, dried shrimp and dried mushrooms are readily available for use.

It often takes foreigners time to adapt to Vietnamese eating and drinking habits. In the main meal, there is usually rice, the indispensable dot is fish sauce. Occasionally there are potatoes, sweet potatoes and other vegetables. Vietnamese food is often spicy, so chili, pepper and garlic are indispensable spices, ginger is also used in many food processing. There are also countless types of herbs and spices used in Vietnamese kitchens.

For those who like to experiment with processing many different dishes, they will discover many interesting things when learning about Vietnamese cuisine. Many foreigners after a long time living and working in Vietnam, when returning to their homeland, the most memorable thing is Vietnamese food.

Dishes No. 1: Chicken Wings Fried Fish Sauce "Drowning" Family Meal

The salty taste of fish sauce when combined with the delicious chicken wings is sure to make an incredibly attractive dish for your family meal. Instead of traditional chicken processing ways, why not try a creative cooking like this?

Ingredient
- 500 grams of chicken wings
- 11 teaspoons of fish sauce
- 1/3 tsp pepper
- 1 purple Onion
- 7 teaspoons white sugar
- 1/3 tsp seasoning
- 1/2 Garlic
- Cooking oil.

Guide

Step 1: Rinse chicken wings, lightly scrub salt on bumps and rinse under water to remove odors. Cut in elbow joints or into small pieces at your discretion.

Step 2: Put chicken wings in bowl, marinated with seasoning, 1 teaspoon sugar, 2 teaspoons of fish sauce. Marinated for about 15 minutes.

Step 3: Onion shelled chopped. Garlic Peel chopped A little, a little to raw timezone.

Step 4: Phase 3 tbsp of fish sauce, 2 teaspoons of sugar, 1/3 tsp pepper and stir until dissolved.

Step 5: Give oil to pan, wait hot then give chicken wings into fried gold for about 15-20 minutes. Picked up the paper to saturate the oil. Then give garlic to the non-scented pan to separate.

Step 6: Pour the oil, leave a little, and then give the shallot hash into the non-scented pan, followed by the chicken and garlic was unscented in the same stir. Then pour the sauce to fry about 3-4 minutes to turn off the stove.

Step 7: Ladle fried chicken wing sauce to the plate, decorate chili peppers or cilantro for beautiful eyes!

Dishes No. 2: How To Cook Korean Hot Kimchi Delicious

Kimchi is a traditional dish that has been loved by the eastern people of South Korea. In winter, Koreans often cook Kimchi with meat and tofu to make the soup hot, warm and extremely nutritious. Is it cold like this that eats a bowl of hot rice with Kimchi soup, what else is it? Let's get in the kitchen to make this delicious and attractive flavor.

Ingredient
· 500 grams of kimchi and cabbage
· 226 grams of pork
· 300 grams of tofu
· 600 ml water
· 2 green onion trees
· 3 tbsp Gochugaru chilli powder
· 1 tablespoon sesame oil
· 1 tablespoon of sauce
· 1 tablespoon minced garlic
· 1-2 tsp sugar
Black pepper
Guide

Step 1: Cut kimchi into pieces of 2 cm long.
Step 2: Cut meat by size with kimchi. cut Tofu pieces thick 1cm, green onion wash, cut long track with kimchi.

Step 3: For pork, kimchi, chili powder, pepper, sesame oil into the cellar, stir fry until the meat is no longer red.
Step 4: For filtered water, sauce, garlic in the pot, boil the heat. Ninh Canh for about 10 minutes. After 10 minutes turn off the stove, leave the pot on the stove to get cooked with steam.
Step 5: After the soup is exhausted, it can be easy to open the lid for tofu and onions. Then cover and tunnel for five more minutes.

Dishes No. 3: Pesto Fried Shrimp With Garlic And Nutritious Potatoes

The rich shrimp, filled with flavor when combined with potatoes and garlic will bring a dish not only incredibly attractive, good boom but also extremely full of nutrients, healthy. In particular, this dish also has a special emphasis on pesto sauce which is extremely good for health and appetite. Don't even save this one-of-a-two formula and get a fortune!

Ingredient
· 285 grams of tiger prawn
· 340 grams of potatoes
· 56 grams of red onion
· 113 grams cherry tomatoes
· 56 grams of vegetable and hair
· 10 grams of parsley
· 10 grams garlic
· 28 grams of walnut
· 35 grams of Parmesan cheese
· 1 tablespoon rice vinegar.

Guide

Step 1: Heating furnace at 450 °f. Rinse and drained of fish raw materials. Cut the potatoes into small pieces just eat. On a baking tray, the stir well is potato with 1 tbsp of cooking oil and seasoning with salt and pepper. Bake for about 25-28 minutes until the ripe potatoes, yellowish brown.

Step 2: Shredded parsley. Chopped walnuts. Minced garlic. Cut the tomato double. Rinse the shrimp and use lightly absorbent paper.
Step 3: In a large bowl, mix parsley, walnut, cheese, 1 tablespoon of vinegar with 2 tablespoons of oil. Wedge with 1/2 tablespoons of salt and pepper. To separate the party.
Step 4: Heat the anti-stick pan over medium heat. When the pan is hot, for 1 tablespoon of oil, then let the onion chopped into. The stir well is hand in 8-10 minutes until the yellow onion is ripe for tomatoes, shrimp and garlic. Occasionally the stir well is hand in 4-5 minutes until the tomato is tender and the shrimp turns pink.
Step 5: When the potatoes have been baked, fill the bowl with the sauce mixed. Add chopped vegetables and gently mix well.
Step 6: Divide the potato part with the sauce off the plates, then the shrimp folded up is completed.

Dishes No. 4: The Recipe Of Shrimp Sauce With An Irresistible Creamy Aroma

Spaghetti with cream sauce is one of the distinctive features that can not be mentioned by beautiful Italian cuisine. The noodles are big, tough served with the sauce, the fragrant and delicious, the ultimate charm is certainly a combination of charm, can conquer the most discerning customers. With this simple recipe, you will be able to grasp the best creamy pasta recipes to treat the whole family.

Ingredient
- 80 grams of spaghetti
- 80 ml cream Whipping
- 150 grams of shrimp
- 40 ml sugar-fresh milk
- 1 tablespoon of parmesan cheese powder
- 1 tablespoon cheddar cheese
- 10 grams butter
- Coriander
- Salt
- Peppercorn

Guide

Step 1: Remove shrimp shells, cut only the back and bring marinated with salt for eating, for about 5 minutes for shrimp to permeate. Cheddar cheese, fibrous. Chopped a little garlic.

Step 2: Boiling water, give spaghetti to boil along with 1 little salt, until the cooked noodles are picked out.

Step 3: Heat the pan, let the butter into the melt and add to the minced garlic for aromatic, then give shrimp into cooked fry.

Step 4: Add the raw milk and whipping cream, cook till boiling, give 2 kinds of parmesan and cheddar cheese, and melt the cheese. Tasting seasoning with 1 little salt pepper for eating.

Step 5: Give pasta to the stir well evenly, noodle sauce turn off the stove.

Step 6: Give out the noodles, sprinkle with coriander, which can be decorated with pepper and shredded cheese.

Dishes No. 5: Quail Eggs Fry Me Snacks Extreme Fun Mouth

The quail egg that was fried with me has long become one of the most popular snacks in last time. However, due to the busy time that we are not always able to carry on and out to enjoy this dish. So why not get your own hands on the kitchen cooking? Saving time, saving the cost is extremely delicious, clean, safe, egg noodles stir fry this cooking will help your meal become more delicious.

Ingredient
· 30 quail eggs
· 100 gram Me ripe
· 200 grams of roasted camel
· 3 teaspoons of fish sauce
· 3 teaspoons sugar
· 1/2 tsp msg
· Vegetables
· Chili Peppers
Garlic
Guide

Step 1: Rinse quail eggs and boil cooked. Cooked eggs, gently picked out, peel off the crust so that eggs are not crushed.

Step 2: Let me in warm water soak for about 15 minutes. Then picked out, crushed and then filtered to take the water essence. Unconfirmed.

Step 3: Non-aromatic garlic minced and sour water into the boil, **then** add sugar, fish sauce, seasoning.

Step 4: Continue the boil until the tamarind sauce makes me a fever, and the quail egg is peeled. Using chopsticks stir well is gentle, lest eggs are crushed.

Step 5: For a while for the egg to warm spices then turn off the stove.

Step 6: Give the egg to the plate, pour the other sauce up. Sprinkle more peanuts (batter is the best), fresh peppers and coriander are washed and enjoyed.

Dishes No. 6: Stir-Fried Squid With Rich Compote Sauce

Stir-fried squid is the favorite dish of many people by crispy taste, delicious and attractive. Combined with the rich sauce, the dish will become outstanding and excellent, making you not resist to eat a piece more.

Ingredient
- 3 cuttlefish
- 400 grams cherry tomatoes
- 1.5 red onion
- 2 garlic tpress
- 1.5 peppers
- 2 holding mint leaves
- 3 pinch dried pepper
- 2.5 Lemon Gold
- 7 tablespoons olive oil
- 1 tablespoon balsamic vinegar
- 2 teaspoons of honey
- 3 tbsp. sauce
- 1 tablespoon rice vinegar
- 2 teaspoons of sesame oil
- 1 tablespoon coriander seeds

- 2 tablespoons roasted sesame seeds
- Salt
- Pepper

Guide

Step 1: Preliminary processing of raw materials: squeezed lemon juice, chopped garlic and chili peppers. Rinse, chopped mint leaves and cherry tomatoes. Chopped onions.

Step 2: Cut off the tentacles cuttle-fish and clean the cuttle-fish. You can ask the salesperson to do it always in the market to help lose time.

Step 3: Get 3 tablespoons of olive oil, stir up the cuttle-fish along with salt and black pepper for eating. Heat the baking pan, give cuttle-fish to the grill every face about 30 seconds or 1 minute. Then let aside.

Step 4: Make compote sauce: Heat a tablespoon of olive oil, add half of the chopped red onion and coriander seed to the stir well in the pan for about 3-4 minutes, or until tender but not yellowish brown.

Step 5: Chopped 1 garlic and 1 chili. Give 1 garlic and 1 pinch the dried chili Peppers to 1 minute, then add a fresh chili in 1-2 minutes. Add balsamic vinegar and 1 lemon juice to stir well.

Step 6: Take the pan from the stove, for 1 half of the chopped onion left. Give 300 grams of sliced cherry tomatoes and 2 tablespoons of olive oil. Let's cool down 1 mint in the mix.

Step 7: Make salsa sauce: give 2 tablespoons of olive oil, 100 grams of cherry tomatoes, 1 half onion, pepper, 1 holding remaining mint leaves, 1 lemon juice and 1 minced pepper in a small bowl, mix well with salt and black pepper grinding.

Step 8: Make sauce: for honey, soy sauce, rice wine vinegar, sesame oil and half-lemon juice in a small bowl and mix until mixture blends well. Add 1 pinch of dried pepper, 1 chopped minced garlic, roasted sesame seed to mix well.

Step 9: Full-plate compote sauce, level up and then pour the salsa sauce over cuttle-fish. Served with prepared sauce is given.

Dishes No. 7: Stir-Fried Seafood With Cucumber And Cool Medium

A simple yet extremely explosive, rich, attractive flavor of seafood dishes from the ocean. Besides, the cucumber has a cool, soothing scent that will balance the nutritional ingredients for the dish, so that your body is delivering so much energy for a long working day. Easy to do, convenient to taste, nutritious, guilt without entering the kitchen right?

Ingredient
· 300 grams of tiger prawn
· 300 grams squid
· 4 Scallops
· 2 cucumbers
· 2 onion Bulbs
· 2 red peppers
· 2 garlic tpress
· 1 tablespoon shrimp sauce
· 2 teaspoons brown sugar
· 3 citrus fruits
· 1 tablespoon fish sauce
· Cooking oil

· Mint leaves
Coriander
Guide
Step 1: Preliminary shrimp processing (if necessary) and chopped cuttle-fish into edible pieces, separate the tentacles to intact. Cut scallops in pairs.
Step 2: Cut chopped onions, the white part into the rings and the blue part into the diagonal slice, wider. Cut the cucumber in double vertical, scraping all the cucumber seeds with water.
Step 3: Cut cucumber into long pieces, chopped garlic and 1 chili. The peppers rest sliced, and then add the lemon.
Step 4: North Pan up the stove, to fire big. Add cooking oil and shrimp sauce. Fry real fast for about 1 minute or so, then add small cut red peppers, garlic and onions.
Step 5: Continue to fry the stir well evenly mixed in a minute and add cucumber, fish sauce, sugar and juice of a lemon.
Step 6: Add seafood to the stir well in 2 minutes, until the ingredients are ripe.
Step 7: Ladle dish out bowl, decorate with sliced chili, green onion and half lemon. So is the finished dish.

Dishes No. 8: The Eggs Are Just Bold And Delicious Ideal

The braised egg dish brings a bold, attractive flavor that does not lose any savory dishes. This will be the perfect choice when you have the little "Crave" something really bold but do not want to be in the kitchen stove or outside the meal eat expensive meals. With this egg depot, you can eat with steamed rice, noodles or some vegetables to make a salad!

Ingredient
· 7 chicken Eggs
· 4 tbsp. sauce
· 1 teaspoon sugar
· 1 teaspoon salt
· 1/2 tsp pepper
· 2 anise flowers
· 2 laurel leaves
Peppercorn
500 ml water

Guide
Step 1: Give the egg to the pot, pour cold water to the egg and boil until the egg matures. Prepare 1 bowl of

cold water, ripe eggs picked out, drop right into the bowl of cold water for about 15 minutes. After soaking about 15 minutes, peel the egg and separate the bowl.

Step 2: Mix evenly 500 ml of water, 4 tablespoons of sauce, 1 teaspoon of sugar, 1 teaspoon of salt, 1/2 teaspoon of pepper, 2 flower anise, 2 laurel leaves and then boil, then tighten the fire.
Step 3: When the boil rolls up, drop the egg into the warehouse on a small heat for about 20 minutes, turn off the fire, wait cool and enjoy.

Dishes No. 9: Steamed Noodle Soup No One Is Irresistible

Rice noodles are quite popular in Vietnamese cuisine and are preferred by many. With this recipe, you will be able to make homemade noodles super-attractive at home but still ensure delicious taste, attractive not lose any restaurant. No more hesitation, isn't it?

Ingredient
· 400 grams bone tubing
· 500 grams of rib tenderloin
· 100 grams of magnolia
· 100 grams of sandalwood
· 500 grams of noodles
· 100 grams of raw spring
· Green onion
· Coriander
·Bean sprouts

Guide
Step 1: Rinse the bone and then boil through, then rinse with water and then take the broth. Tunnel bone with 1 tablespoon of salt, 2 tablespoons of seasoning.

Pay attention to clear the foam that emerged during the process of tunnel bone to the broth and tasty.

Step 2: Rinse the ribs, boil it and rinse well. Continue to marinate with 1/2 teaspoons of salt, 1 teaspoon of seasoning, half a teaspoon of powder for about 10 minutes.

Step 3: Carpentry, mushrooms cut off root, soak in hot water for hatch and rinse, drained, chopped.

Step 4: Mix magnolia, mushroom, green onion with a small spring. Tablet into each small member, and then drop in boiled broth. Until the surface of the water is ripe, picked up.

Step 5: Non-aromatic onions and for the pork ribs in stir-fry, the stir well will all be poured into broth. Seasoning tasting added spices for the broth to eat. Non-aromatic onions for a dry to sprinkle with noodles grow when eating.

Step 6: Quilted with hot water and then drain. Spread the rice noodles, add a rib and salvage it to the top, and use it, sprinkle with more green onions, coriander and non-aromatic dried onion to complete.

Dishes No. 10: Pork And Coconut Eggs Melt In The Mouth

This egg dish, especially in pieces of meat marinated with chili, onions, garlic thoroughly, makes the flavor extremely strong and irresistible for the dish. After the cellar in coconut water, the meat dish will be soft and delicious so that the melting in the mouth, bringing the attractive dish makes any food must be bewitching. With this recipe of coconut egg Depot, surely your family's feast will be more attractive than the mess.

Ingredient
· 500 grams of bacon
· 500 grams of pork leg
· 3 tablespoons vegetable oil
· 1 liter of coconut water
· 3 tbsp. fish sauce
· 8 eggs
· 3 red peppers
· 2 bird's eye chili
· 8 leaf shallot
· 8 Garlic tpress
· 1 lemon

- 1 tablespoon sand sugar
- 1 teaspoon salt
- 500 gram sugar
150 ml water

Guide

Step 1: Cut bacon, Meat loaf into 5 cm segments. Boiled egg, peeled. Chopped bird's eye chili, shallot and garlic. Squeeze 1 lemon juice.

Step 2: Give pork to bowl with bird's eye chili, shallot, garlic, lemon juice, sand sugar and salt. Mix evenly into the meat and to marinate overnight.

Step 3: 500 gram of sugar and 125 ml of water in the pan over medium heat, stirring slowly until sugar completely melt. Downgrade to medium heat for 10 minutes, when the mixture is slightly dense, it slowly pour 125 ml of water left in and stir well. Cook an additional 5 minutes for a mixture of dense and dark red colors. Turn off the stove, pour the caramel mixture out to cool jars.

Step 4: Heat the oil in a pan with large fire until reaching 190 degrees Celsius.

Step 5: Let pork marinated into the pan along with 2 teaspoons of caramel sauce. The stir well is hands-on for about 4 minutes until the caramel sauce marinated.

Step 6: Pour coconut water and 300 ml water into the boil. The impurities and excess spices surface to retain water. Fire and heat for 2 hours.

Step 7: Add fish sauce, eggs and 3 chili Peppers to a 1-hours more fire.

Step 8: Remove the pan from the stove, fry out the plate and enjoy the pickles, steamed rice and chili sauce.

Dishes No. 11: Rolls Of Vegetables With A Delicious And Breathtaking

Rolls have long been a familiar dish, but when used only to multiply vegetables, the dish will become more delicious, hard to resist. For vegetarians or sisters who want to lose weight, this dish has just supplied enough nutrients, low fat, extremely good for health. Let's just save the recipe rolls with this super unique vegetable.
Ingredient
· 1 set of Rolls
· 1/2 cabbage
· 1 soybean
· 1/2 Carrot
· 2 garlic tpress
· 1 ginger
· 1 tablespoon coriander
· 2 tablespoons sesame oil
· 1 rice wine soup
· 1 tablespoon of sauce
· 3 teaspoons corn flour
· Salt
· Cooking oil

Guide

Step 1: Rinse vegetables, chopped cabbage, sliced carrot into long strands. Chopped ginger and garlic.

Step 2: Heat the sesame oil on the pan with large fire, then add cabbage, carrots, soybean to the stir well evenly in 1 minute.

Step 3: Add garlic and ginger to fry for a few more minutes, until the ingredients are tender, then add the sauce, rice wine, leaf onions and coriander to the stir well equally.

Step 4: Pour out the bowl dish mixture for cold, reduce excess fat.

Step 5: Put a piece of rolls on a flat, clean surface, a head towards yourself. Mix corn flour with 3 tablespoons of water.

Step 6: Spoon a teaspoon of freshly cooked vegetables into the corner of rolls and paper rolls. When scrolling to the middle, double the side of the paper, spread the corn flour mixture with water on the remaining paper to hold the rolls for sure.

Step 7: Full Roll of the remaining vegetable mixture.

Step 8: Pour oil into the pan, heated to 180 degrees Celsius. Oil-frying Rolls for 2 – 3 minutes, until the crust is ripe, brown. Then enjoy now.

Dishes No. 12: Re-Lemon Beef Salad

Re-lemon beef salad is an appetizers of many guests by the fresh flavor of vegetables and meat, which offers sweet and sweet sour taste. Re-lemon beef salad is often used as a target for parties.

Ingredient
· 450 grams of beef
· Lettuce, salad
· Chilli hash
· Minced garlic
· Purple Onion
· 1 carrot
· Lemon
· 10 grams of peanut
· Salt, sugar
· Fish sauce, sesame oil
· Vinegar, seasoning
· 1 teaspoon non-African coffee
· 10 grams of fried crackers

Guide

Step 1: Heat pan and peanut into ripe roast. Make a bowl of sugar, and then rinse and clean.

Step 2: Boil the oil and give the chips to fry. Next, peel the carrot and rinse it after it, give it to the carrot bowl a little soft squeeze salt and rinse it with water it is an important step in the way of re-lemon, squeeze the carrot with salt will help the carrot less pungent and easy to eat.

Step 3: Continue to make sauce by mixing raw materials is garlic minced, lemon juice, vinegar, seasoning, salt, fish sauce, sugar, sesame oil.

Step 4: Clean and sliced beef, it is possible to replace the beef meat for a more delicious fresh lemon refresher. Boil a pot of water and let the cow last.

Step 5: Mix beef re-lemon salad: for carrot, onion, shallot, beef in one bowl, then pour the sauce in and squeeze 1 lemon. Mix well, squeeze the beef.

lemons, and then the lettuce, onion and peanuts. Decorate a few slices of fresh lemon, savour lemon steak with crispy crackers.

Dishes No. 13: Stir Fried Shrimp With Low-Calorie Asparagus, Just Keep The Shape Perfect

Fried shrimp with asparagus is a nutrient full of nutrients, and proteins have rich in vitamins and minerals that are beneficial to the body. Moreover, the dish has a calorie of less than 300 kcal. Just delicious, beautiful and not worried about fat, nothing more perfect for her menu.

Ingredient
· 445 grams of shrimp
· 445 grams of asparagus
· 4 tablespoons olive oil
· 1 teaspoon salt
· 1/2 tsp red pepper
· 1 teaspoon garlic
· 1 teaspoon ginger
· 1 tablespoon fish sauce
2 tbsp. lime juice
Guide

Step 1: Heat 2 tablespoons olive oil on frying pan. Chopped ginger and garlic.
Step 2: Preliminary shrimp and shrimp in a frying pan, add 1/2 tablespoons of salt and red pepper to flavor the taste. Until the shrimp rose, they are removed from the pan.

Step 3: Warm up to 2 tbsp of remaining olive oil. Rinse the asparagus, cut off the stalk and cut twice, then give it to the frying pan.
Step 4: Add ginger, chopped garlic, for 1/2 tablespoons remaining salt. The stir well was hands-on when the asparagus was slightly crispy.
Step 5: Add shrimp to stir-fry with asparagus, extra fish sauce. The stir well is hands-on until the ingredients are cooked spices and ripe.
Step 6: When the ingredients are ripe, add lime juice, an stir well once and turn off the stove. The dish you can enjoy.

Dishes No. 14: Stir Fried Shrimp With Lemon Garlic

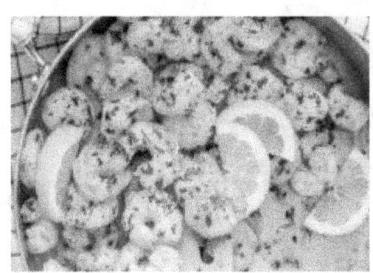

The crispy, greasy prawns of garlic butter, combined with a slight spicy and sour taste of lime will make you faint from the first bite. This dish is very easy to do, it only takes very little time in the kitchen. Let's get your hands in the kitchen right away, surely this recipe won't disappoint you.

Ingredient
· 3 tbsp butter
· 455 grams of shrimp
· 1 teaspoon salt
· 1/2 tsp pepper
· 3 garlic tpress
· 1/2 tsp chili powder
· 1 tablespoon parsley
3 tbsp. lime juice

Guide

Step 1: Preliminary shrimp, left head and tail shrimp. Chopped garlic and parsley.

Step 2: North Pan onto the stove, to medium heat, for butter until flowing. Rate the shrimp on the pan so that the shrimp do not overlap. Sprinkle salt and pepper it up, let alone when the underside of red shrimp is overturned.

Step 3: Add garlic, chili powder to the stir well evenly. Continue for the parsley, all stir well.

Step 4: Add lime juice, the stir well really quickly hands off the stove.

Step 5: After completion, the shrimp will have a beautiful ripe red color, striking with parsley leaves, aromatic coriander butter. Now you can enjoy it.

Dishes No. 15: Garlic Pasta Spaghetti

Do not hesitate to go to the kitchen and make a pasta with garlic Shrimp Super simple This nutrient rich? Surely the smell of the tough noodles and the attractive flavor of shrimp and garlic flavor will knock you down from the first try.

Ingredient
· 450 grams of shrimp
· 225 grams of spaghetti
· 10 grams of parsley
· 3 tbsp butter
· 3 garlic tpress
· 1 teaspoon salt
· 1 teaspoon pepper
· 1 teaspoon chili powder
· 1/2 Lemon

Guide

Step 1: Chopped garlic and parsley. Remove the shrimp shells. Boil cooked pasta.

Step 2: Put the pot on the stove, to medium heat. Let butter in to butter melt out in the pot.

Step 3: Give garlic to fry until ripe gold. Add shrimp, salt and pepper, stir-fry until shrimp cooked, colored pink orange.

Step 4: Add the juice of half the lemon, chili powder and parsley to the stir well evenly.

Step 5: Continue to add pasta, stir well until the ingredients have blended together. Feed the plates and enjoy it.

Dishes No. 16: Vegetarian Rice Recipe With Rich And Nutritious Vegetables

For vegetarians, this vegetable roasted rice will surely be an indispensable dish in the daily menu. Just rich in nutrients, good for health, rich and delicious, very easy to do, but do not hesitate to get your hands in the kitchen right now?

Ingredient
· 60 grams of carrots
· 75 grams of onion
· 50 grams bell pepper
· 75 grams of broccoli
· 60 grams of corn
· 75 grams of peas
· 3 eggs
· 690 grams of steamed rice
· 1 garlic
· 2 tablespoons fish sauce
· 1 teaspoon sesame oil
· 1 teaspoon cooking oil
· Pepper

Guide

Step 1: Rinse then diced carrot seed; Sliced onion, bell pepper. Chopped garlic, hit three eggs.

Step 2: Give oil to pan, to fire to, fry carrots, onions and garlic for the ripening.
Step 3: Add bell peppers and broccoli, stir about 3-4 minutes.
Step 4: Give the egg into the stir well with vegetables, cooked eggs for steamed rice to the stir well until all the ingredients mix well.
Step 5: Add peas, corn, fish sauce, sesame oil and pepper into the pan. Continue to the stir well when the vegetables are ripe, crispy and rich rice. Now make a plate and enjoy it.

Dishes No. 17: Full Sweet And Sour Vegetarian Noodle

Thick, tough, rich flavors of delicious spices, attractive, sweet and sour yakisoba is the ideal choice for a fast and fully nutritious lunch. If you're wondering what a lunch now is, refer to this super-convenient noodle recipe now!

Ingredient
· 240 grams of yakisoba noodles
· 120 grams of red cabbage
· 2 carrots
· 30 grams of coconut milk cashew
· 1 ginger
· 2 garlic tpress
· 1 bundle of green onions
· 1 Chili
· 1 tablespoon corn flour
· 5 teaspoons of Sherry vinegar
· 2 tbsp. Orange Jam
4 tbsp. fish sauce
Guide

Step 1: Rinse and wipe the whole raw material. Take a medium pot, give water to the boil. Cut red cabbage yarn.

Step 2: Peel the ginger, then hash or grind. Peel the carrot, then slice it thin. Garlic also sliced thin. Slice the green onions, divide the leaves and separate the white tubercle. Chopped peppers, dropped nuts.
Step 3: Mix soysauce, vinegar, jam, 60 ml of water and corn flour in a small bowl. To cross a party.
Step 4: When boiling water, separate the noodles into cook for about 2 minutes until tender. Drain the water, then rinse in a sink under cool water. Mix with a drop of cooking oil and let aside.
Step 5: Cut cashew nuts into small chips.
Step 6: Heat a little oil in a large skillet to fire. Add garlic, ginger, green onions, coriander and a half of chili peppers to the stir well in khoa4rng 30 seconds until scented. Give the cabbage and carrots to the stir well for about 3-5 minutes, until soft cabbage is given.
Step 7: Give noodles into the pan. Mix all noodles with other ingredients. Pour the sauce mixture into the stir well again until the sauce is mixed with noodles.
Step 8: Take the pan from the stove, pitching noodles. Sprinkle the cashew nuts up and enjoy.

Dishes No. 18: Aromatic Chicken Soup For Winter Tonic

The chicken soup is simple, easy to rework is delicious and bold. On monsoon days, your family meal will become warm, tasty, and more cheerful when you enjoy chicken soup with hot rice. Let's save this recipe and give it a fortune.

Ingredient
- 455 grams minced chicken meat
- 25 grams of deep-fried flour
- 1 egg
- 55 grams of shredded Parmesan cheese
- 4 garlic tpress
- 10 grams parsley
- 1 teaspoon salt
- 1/2 tsp pepper
- 2 tablespoons cooking oil
- 60 grams of carrots
- 110 grams celery
- 150 grams of onion
- 1.9 liters of chicken broth
- 1 Laurel Leaf

1 tablespoon lemon juice

Guide

Step 1: In a medium bowl, mix crushed chicken, crispy flour, egg, parmesan cheese, 2 garlic juice and parsley chopped with salt and pepper. Mix hands and then park the meat balls by about 2 cm.

Step 2: Put the pot on the stove, heat 1 tablespoon cooking oil with medium heat. Give the meat a fry for about 4-5 minutes, until ripe, yellowish brown is. Let the meat aside.

Step 3: Warm up 1 tablespoon leftodish oil. For onions, carrots, and celery has chopped, occasionally the stir well is hand until the vegetables are tender. Add 2 chopped garlic squeeze to the stir well for 1-2 minutes until the smell wakes.

Step 4: Pour chicken broth and give the laurel leaves in, cover, boil till boiling.

Step 5: When boiling water, add chicken made to simmer for fire from 7-8 minutes longer.

Step 6: Add some Parmesan cheese to taste if you want, and then taste the seasoning and pepper to eat. So, your soup is done.

Dishes No. 19: Salad Thai Chicken Carrots Are Protein And Good For Health

A salad plate with delicious chicken pieces, an extremely attractive Thai-style explosion, combined with healthy green vegetables, will bring a charming, hard-to-be-irresistible dish. The Thai style of salad dressing also makes you look to the last piece of the sauce. Not only that, the nutritional components are extremely balanced, help you not only add healthy but also remove excess fat effectively.

Ingredient
- 4 non-skinned chicken breast
- 1 bunch of baby carrots
- 1 box of bulbs
- 1 salad
- 1/2 Cucumber
- 1 green pepper
- 1/2 bunch of coriander
- 1/2 bundle of mint leaves
- 1 pinch fresh ginger
- 1 lemongrass
- 1/2 Lemon

- 1 tablespoon red curry sauce
- 1 tablespoon miso sauce
- 1 tablespoon coconut milk
- 2 tablespoons fish sauce
- 1 tablespoon palm sugar
- 100 ml rice vinegar
- 1 teaspoon peanut butter
- Black pepper

Sauce

Guide

Step 1: Heat oven to 180 degrees Celsius.

Step 2: Mix curry sauce, miso sauce, coconut milk and 1 less real pepper and spread over the chicken breast. Put the chicken in the baking tray, bake for 10-12 minutes until the chicken drains out. Get the chicken out of the oven and let aside.

Step 3: Remove the peel, grated cucumber into long pieces. Give the cucumber to the bowl, marinated with a little sauce and let it saddle for 5 minutes, then rinse and dry.

Step 4: Remove the bark, cut carrots according to the strands. Pomegranate seeds.

Step 5: Make a salad dressing by removing the peel and then pounding ginger with lemongrass. Chopped, remove the green pepper seeds. Mix it all with fish sauce, rice vinegar, juice of 1/2 lemon and palm sugar until completely thawed sugar.

Step 6: Rinse, separate the lettuce leaves. Stack chicken off the plate, decorate the surrounding vegetables.

Pour the sauce and sprinkle with the little cut energy on top and enjoy.

Dishes No. 20: Cook Delicious Eel Vermicelli Is No Less Than A Restaurant

Eel vermicelli is a dish with very high nutritional content, rich in protein, fat, and vitamins. Eel meat also works to foster blood, eliminate rheumatism, can cure malnutrition, dysentery, backache, internal hemorrhoids, rheumatism ... A bowl of hot, delicious eel noodles is just as good for health, isn't it?

Ingredient
- 500 grams of Fresh Eel
- 200 grams of dried vermicelli
- 300 grams Bean sprouts
- 35 grams of Cornstarch
- 1 tangle of laksa leaves
- 1/2 Onion
- 3 Onions
- 1 Ginger
- Salt
- Edible oil
- Reduce
- Gallopia

Vinegar or lemon
Guide

Step 1: For raw eel, put the eel in a pot, sprinkle with grain salt and then swing up some shock until the eel is no longer viscous, no more throwing.

Step 2: Squeeze the eel with your hands once more, then wash off the mucus with water. Squeeze a little vinegar or lemon into squeeze thoroughly to remove all the oil and wash again with water to clean.

Step 3: Put the eel's head into a pointed stick to hold the eel in place, use a sharp knife to peck the eel's body, use the hand to brake the eel's belly and continue to slide the knife down, then gently remove bone. Cut off the head, separate the bones, head and eel meat in 2 separate bowls. Avoid using eel wash water now to avoid being fishy.

Step 4: If the eel is small, leave it alone; If the eel is large, cut the eel into long strips. Then marinate the eel with a little salt and pepper for 10 minutes to infuse and then add the cornstarch to the suspension.

Step 5: Wash laksa leaves, bean sprouts and onions. Cut the onion into long fibers.

Step 6: Soak vermicelli in water for 5-10 minutes to soften vermicelli.

Step 7: Put the eel head and bone in a pot of boiling water with onion and grilled ginger. Season with salt to taste. When the water starts to boil, lower the heat to a simmer and remove all the floating bubbles so that the water is clear.

Step 8: North frying pan on the stove, flooding oil for 4-5cm. Add each batch of eel and fry until the eel is dark yellow. Put the eel out and drain the oil.

Step 9: Put bean sprouts, onions and laksa leaves in a bowl, soak the noodles in the boiling water to soften them to top, then dry the eel in and then use the broth. Finally sprinkle a little onion on top to be eaten immediately.

Dishes No. 21: Nikujaga - Beef Stew With Japanese Potatoes

This nikujaga is the perfect choice for cold winter days. Beef stew with sweet potatoes, combined with frugal vegetables, good for health, creating a rich, attractive flavor, this dish will make your family's meal more rejuvenated. , warm and delicious. Save the recipe for super-charming winter wonderland of cherry blossom country.

Ingredient
·400 grams Beef
·750 grams of Potatoes
·10 Snow peas
·2 Onions
·1 carrot
·1 teaspoon Cooking oil
·400 ml Dashi soy sauce
·4 tbsp Sugar
· 1/2 tsp Salt
·4 tbsp Soy sauce
·2 tablespoons sake
·2 tbsp Mirin

· Green leaves

Guide

Step 1: Bare through snow peas with boiling water for 1 minute, then soak in ice water to cool. Remove the water, cut the beans diagonally into 2-3 pieces and then separate.
Step 2: Rinse, peel and chop potatoes, carrots into small pieces to taste. Remove the peel, cut the onion into small pieces.
Step 3: Cut the beef into thin slices, about 5mm thick.
Step 4: Heat the oil in a pan, stir fry the beef until it is cooked, brown.
Step 5: Add potatoes, carrots, and onions to the stir well for a few minutes.
Step 6: Pour in dashi sauce, cover and cook for 15 minutes on medium heat until the potatoes are soft. Note that in this step, do not stir.
Step 7: In another bowl, mix sugar, soy sauce, mirin, sake, salt and place in a pan. Cook for about 5 - 10 minutes.
Step 8: Turn off the stove, remove the pan from the stove. Let the food cool for 30 minutes. Add snow peas, sprinkle green onions and serve with hot rice or noodles. Can be reheated for a little hot if desired.

Dishes No. 22: Charming, Attractive With The Well-Diced Beef

Shaking beef is a familiar dish made from Vietnamese beef, inspired by the magnificent and impressive French cuisine. This will be an extremely ideal dish for you to enjoy with your family on the monsoon. What are you waiting for, don't go to the kitchen right away.

Ingredient
- 910 grams Thick ribs, boneless
- 10 cloves of Garlic
- 3 tbsp Brown sugar
- 5 tbsp Soy sauce
- 2 tbsp Oyster sauce
- 1 tbsp Fish sauce
- 1 tbsp Granulated sugar
- 2 tbsp White vinegar
- 2 tbsp Water
- 1 red onion
- 2 bunch watercress
- 3 Tomatoes
- 2 tbsp Vegetable oil
- Black pepper

Guide

Step 1: Minced garlic, slice onion. Cut the beef into small pieces to eat.

Step 2: In a large bowl, combine beef with garlic, brown sugar, 3 tablespoons soy sauce, oyster sauce, fish sauce and black pepper. Stir the beef to season and marinate at room temperature for 30 minutes.

Step 3: In another bowl, mix granulated sugar, 2 tablespoons soy sauce, white vinegar and water together. Add red onion slices to the mixture to soak.

Step 4: Wash and slice tomatoes. Then put the watercress and tomatoes on a plate so beautifully.

Step 5: Heat the pan over high heat, then add the vegetable oil. When the oil starts to boil, rotate the pan to coat the parts of the pan evenly. Add half of the beef and then stir well, shaking the pan, until the meat is slightly burnt and medium cooked (3-5 minutes). Set aside and repeat with remaining beef.

Step 6: Put beef on top of watercress and tomatoes. Garnish with fresh cilantro and pickled red onion. Adding some hot rice is perfect for your family's meal.

Dishes No. 23: Crab Vermicelli Becomes Very Easy To Make With This Recipe

Crab vermicelli is a familiar dish of Vietnamese in general and Northern people in particular with a strong, delicious and attractive flavor. What could be better than going to the kitchen by yourself to make delicious crab vermicelli and crab noodles, which are safe and hygienic?

Ingredient
·1 kg Noodles
·600 grams Copper Crab
·100 grams of Ground Meat
·50 grams Dried shrimp
·2 Chicken eggs
·Peanut
· Green leaves
· Tomatoes
·Dried onion
·Shrimp paste
· Vinegar
Spices, chili

Guide

Step 1: Wash through tofu and cut into pieces, then fry gold. Chopped green onion. Tomatoes cut into areca zone, sauteed with vegetable oil.

Step 2: Wash the crab, peel off the crab shell and crab shell. Use a small stick or stick to collect the colored water from the crab's shell. Crush the crab body or grind it with some salt.

Step 3: Pour the crab into a bowl and mix in water, gently squeeze the crab meat to dissolve into the water. Decant gently pour the water and crab meat into the pot. Repeat mixing, squeeze and decant the water about 2 times until only the hardened shell remains.

Step 4: Put a little seasoning (salt, seasoning, main noodles) in a pot of just filtered crab water, then put it on the stove to simmer over medium heat. Stir gently to combine and float the crab, then remove to a separate bowl.

Step 5: Pour the previously sauteed tomatoes into the crab water pot, season the pot of water with 1 tablespoon shrimp sauce or spices to taste, continue to simmer.

Step 6: Dried shrimps soaked in warm water to soften and puree. Add minced meat, egg, minced shrimp, chopped garlic onion and a little seasoning and mix well.

Step 7: Use a spoon to scoop the mixture into the boiling pot of boiling water. When it was almost time to eat, add a bit of vinegar and season with spices to taste.

Step 8: Non-aromatic shallots, then pour the color of crab water into the pan, stir and turn off the stove.

Step 9: Take 1 amount of noodles to eat into a bowl, sprinkle a little onion on top. Combine water crab and water color with onions, accompanied by a plate of raw vegetables that you can enjoy.

Dishes No. 24: Go To The Kitchen To Make A Delicious Nutritious Lotus Seed Chicken Soup

Chicken soup with lotus seeds is a frugal, fresh, easy-to-eat dish, suitable for both adults and children. Not only that, this dish also helps to develop the brain, restore health to the sick and improve significant resistance.

Ingredient
- 300 grams Chicken meat
- 50 grams of dried lotus seed
- 12 pcs Dried shiitake mushrooms
- 1-2 Shallots
- Ginger
- Green leaves
- Cooking oil
- Granules wedge

Fish sauce

Guide

Step 1: Wash chicken, cut pieces, then marinate for 30 minutes with chopped onions, chopped ginger, seasoning seeds, fish sauce (one teaspoon each). Mix well to flavor the chicken.

Step 2: Shiitake washed, soaked in warm water to soften and cut off the legs. Peeled onion, finely chopped. Ginger shaved, sliced. Scallions and coriander washed, chopped.

Step 3: Lotus seeds soak in cold water before 2 hours until soft. Then picked out, washed and drained.

Step 4: North pot on the stove, add the oil, wait for the hot oil, chopped shallots and sliced ginger for aroma. Then, add the marinated chicken until the meat is sure, add a bowl of filtered water to boil. Wait until the water boils, remove the foam, add lotus seeds, shiitake mushrooms, and scallions.

Step 5: Put the saucepan on the stove and cook until the chicken, lotus seeds and mushrooms are all cooked, then season with spices and seeds to taste, then put onions, chopped coriander, and stir for a while. then turn off the heat. Finally, scoop the soup into a bowl and use it while it's still hot to enjoy the freshest taste.

Dishes No. 25: How To Cook Delicious Thai Hot Pot Simply At Home

Thai hot pot with special spicy and sour taste with many fresh ingredients providing nutrients is always a favorite dish of Vietnamese people. At parties, gather friends or rainy days that gather with a Thai hot pot is nothing.

Ingredient
· 1 kg of tubular bone
· 1 kg Clam
· 1 kg of shrimp
· 1 kg of cuttlefish
· Mushrooms
· Banana Corn
· Need vegetables
· Vegetable
· Vegetables
· 6 lemongrass plants
· 1 galangal
· 2 citrus fruits
· Lime leaves
· Sugar

· Seasoning
· Thai hot pot spices
Noodles, rice noodles
Guide
Step 1: Clean the bones of the pipe, then bring to the pot to boil, then wash with water again to clean the bones and dirt. Then add a little salt and water in the bone to the pot and boil the black foam, scoop it out with a spoon and continue simmering on low heat.
Step 2: Pick and wash the morning glory, spinach, celery, mushrooms. Sliced bananas and soaked in water mixed with a little vinegar. Lemongrass peeled off the outer shell, smashing the white head, the body cut short.
Step 3: Shrimp cut off the legs, head, peeled, washed and split back to remove the black thread to reduce the fishy smell. Clams wash and soak in water for diluted salt, add a few slices of chili for about 1 hour to clam off all sandy soil, then wash again. Rinse the squid sliced or cut into bite-sized pieces and then arrange on a plate.
Step 4: Bone broth after boiling, add some lemongrass, crushed galangal and lime leaves to make the broth more fragrant. Season with spices, fish sauce, seasoning seeds, lemon juice and 1 packet of hotpot spices in a pot of water to taste, you can add tomatoes as you like.
Step 5: The pot of hotpot water is done, now all we have to do is set the table. Display vegetables, seafood, noodles, noodles, dipping sauce arranged around, in

the middle of the pot to set a hotpot. When eating, add a little satay and start adding the shrimp, squid, clams to the pot of boiling hot pot and dip with vegetables.

Dishes No. 26: Revealing How To Make Delicious Ribs That Cannot Be Denied

Choosing a dish that is both delicious and nutritious but brings new feelings to the family every day is certainly not a simple thing.

Ingredient
· 500 grams of small rib
· 2 dried onion
· 1 garlic
· Sugar
· Fish sauce
· Cooking oil

Guide

Step 1: Rib after washing you give into the pot, add the boiled water until boiling, turn off the stove, salvage the rib to rinse with clean water, drain.

Step 2: Minced garlic and onions. For a little oil fed into the pot, hot oil for garlic onions in non-aromatic. Golden garlic onions You quickly hand to the ribs, add seasoning and the stir well comes when the rib is fragrant, turn off the stove

Step 3: Make water colored ribs: Take another pot, give the 1/2 tablespoon of filtered water, 1/2 tablespoons of sugar, boil on small heat till the mixture turn colored cockroach wings is being.

Step 4: At this when the mixture is brown wing cockroaches you quickly pour the ribs fry in step 3 into general. The stir well has a very warm rib.

Step 5: Until the rib is soft, you open it if you see more water. The warehouse comes when the water is, turn off the stove and sprinkle in less pepper.

Dishes No. 27: All-Weekend Beef Noodles

As a dish with quite a feat, the beef with wine sauce is delicious, attractive but often not chosen by many people to prepare at home, simple, time-saving, let us together Reference how to do this.

Ingredient
· 500 grams beef
· 1 ginger
· 1 carrot
· 2 potatoes
· 1 garlic
· 1 tomato
· 2 tablespoons tomato sauce
· 1 bowl of wine
· 1 cinnamon rod
· Fish sauce
· Peppercorn
· Seasoning Powder
· The five Flavors
1 tablespoon sugar
Guide

Step 1: Beef washed, cut into large pieces, then boil 1 pot of boiling water, then beef for blanching, take out and wash again.

Step 2: Put beef in a bowl, add fish sauce, salt, pepper, ginger scraped and crushed, 1 min of minced garlic, five spices, sugar, wine, cinnamon then mix well and marinate meat for 40 minutes to infuse spices.

Step 3: Grated carrots, peeled and shaped like a flower, cut into thick pieces. Cut the potatoes into large pieces and rinse well. Diced tomatoes.

Step 4: Put the saucepan on the stove with 2 tablespoons of cooking oil, add the garlic oil until fragrant, add the aroma, then fry the tomatoes until the tomatoes are soft, then pour the marinated beef bowl into the stir fry together.

Step 5: Add tomato sauce and pour boiling water to cover the surface of the meat, then stew for tender cooked beef, add potatoes, carrots to the stew for another 10-15 minutes, season the seasonings to taste and turn off the stove.

Dishes No. 28: Recipe Of Pork Intestine Stuffed With Meat Then Fried

Last week, let's spend some time doing the pork meat stuffed then fried crispy delicious family, friends and loved ones.

Ingredient
· 300 grams of young pigs
· 150 grams of minced meat
· 100 grams of roasted camel
· 1/2 Carrot
· 1 onion
· 5 of the Magnolia
· 5 Mushrooms
· Relish
Green Onion.

Guide

Step 1: The young pig washed, drained vinegar and salt to squeeze, rub and wash the pork and deodorant fishy. The mushroom is soaked in cold water until it is incense, and the fungus is blooming and washed off and chopped; green onion washed, chopped.

Step 2: Carrot peel sliced, then minced, roasted peanuts, rubbed with shells. Then let in bowl include minced meat with mushrooms, green onions, 1/2 tablespoons of soup, 1 teaspoon pepper, 1 teaspoon of oyster oil, 1 teaspoon of msg, 1/2 tablespoons of fish sauce. Combine the ingredients into a uniform mixture.

Step 3: Use a hopper or bottle cap to filter meat in the broth. They are evenly (not too tight) until all ingredients are used to tie the cord. Please fill the soup with a glass.

Step 4: When the cooked pork is used to remove the water then cut the slice and bring fried gold.

When eating chopped pork intestines stuffed into small slices, chili sauce or sour-spicy fish sauce is great.

Dishes No. 29: Grilled Chicken With A Tasty Honey Sauce, Eat The Rice

Grilled chicken wing with honey sauce is rated as one of the delicious flavors of the flavor that the housewife can make for the family to enjoy, this is also the delicious summer day to ensure the strengthening of tastes for the whole house in the hot season There you go.

Ingredient
· 450 grams of chicken wings
· 1 tablespoon pepper coffee
· 1 tablespoon salt coffee
· 15 ml of cooking oil
· 45 grams of butter
· 30 ml of honey
· Chili sauce
· 15 ml of rice wine
· 5 ml soy sauce
· 5 ml Hoisin sauce
2 tablespoons chopped cilantro.
Guide

Step 1: First when grilled chicken wings honey sauce is that you have to heat the oven under temperature of 400 degrees F, then you prepare a big bowl, then remove the chicken wings cleaned in the bowl, pour more pepper, salt along with the oil to bowl and stir the chicken wings to make the spice to warm spices.

Step 2: Next step you get the foil lining above the baking tray, then you've folded the chicken in turn onto the baking tray and let it in the oven that was heated from the front. You bake the chicken wings about 50 minutes, pay attention during the baking process you flip the chicken wings.

Step 3: After the chicken wings are baked cooked, you boil the butter melted in the pan, then remove more alcohol, soy sauce, honey, chili sauce, salt, hosin sauce into the pan, and the stir well heat the mixture up.

Step 4: You minimize the fire and boil the mixture above, then new to the chicken wings in the pan is carrying the boiled sauce, the stir well is all chicken wings until the sauce has been cling to the chicken wings.

Dishes No. 30: How To Make Beef With Tasty Tamarind Sauce As A Restaurant

The tamarind sauce is simple and easy to rework with a hot rice dish. Just a few simple steps, you can have a beef oven with attractive tamarind sauce. Get your hands on it.

Ingredient
· 300 grams of beef
· 100 grams of abalone mushroom
· 100 grams of needle mushroom
· 100 grams of ganoderme mushrooms
· 200 grams water morning glory
· 50 grams of onions
· 15 grams of horned pepper
· 50 grams of tamarind juice
· 40 grams white sugar
· 20 ml of fish sauce
· 20 grams of oyster
· 3 grams of pepper
· 15 grams of purple onion
· 15 grams of garlic

- 10 grams of lemongrass
- 1 Chili

Guide

Step 1: For raw materials on the mill consists of 15gr garlic, 15gr red onion, 10gr lemongrass, 1 chili, 40gr sugar, 20ml fish sauce, 20gr oyster oil, 3gr pepper grinder and indispensable ingredient of 50gr (sappy) water. Finely ground mixture.

Step 2: Cut thin 300gr beef, pour mixture of tamarind sauce, 50gr onion cut with areca bell, 15gr sliced Chili peppers, mix well then marinated with 15 minutes beef to spice up.

Step 3: Prepare a foil-coated pan. The north pan to the stove, to 15 gr vegetable butter, waiting for melted butter, alternating mushrooms and vegetables. Wait when the mushrooms are ripe, the beef marinated in the middle. Root cut mushrooms, soak through salt water 10 minutes before cooking. The vegetables are picked in short, washed and soaked 10 minutes.

Step 4: Beef Just fry just cooked to keep the softness, eaten with bread is very tasty. The rich beef is fragrant with lemongrass garlic, especially the sour taste of tamarind mixed with herbs butter mushrooms that still retain the natural sweetness of brittleness. An aromatic beef saucepan is very attractive, and the family deals on weekend meals are exhausting.

1. Bun Cha (Grilled Pork With Rice Vermicelli Noodle In Dipping Sauce)

Bun Cha originated in Hanoi, Vietnam but it is also a popular dish in other northern cities. After Pho, Bun Cha is seen to be the second classic dishes. The dish can be found at every corner of Hanoi.

Its variant is Bun Thit Nuong in Southern Vietnam, especially in Ho Chi Minh City. The similar points lie in the rice vermicelli noodles, grill porks, green herbs and dipping sauce. But there's a little bit difference between these two. With Hanoi styled dish, vermicelli noodles, grilled pork and herbs are placed separately and only are dipped in a bowl of fully dipping sauce when eating. While in southern styled dish, the noodle and grill meat and herbs and a little of sauce are mixed together in a bowl.

Bun Cha is a vibrant combination of savory and fresh with grilled pork, crisp and green salads, traditional rice vermicelli and a light yet unique dipping sauce. It's an ideal meal for a hot summer.

1. Ingredients (3-4 Servings)

For grilled pork:

- 500g pork belly
- 500g minced shoulder pork
- 50 grams shallots (about 6 – 8 shallots)
- 15 grams garlic (3 – 5 cloves)
- Fish sauce
- Oyster sauce
- Pepper

For pickles:
- 1 Papaya/kohlrabi
- 2 Carrots
- 2 tsp salt
- 2 tbsp vinegar (5% acid)
- 1 tbsp sugar

For dipping sauce:
- 1 cup fish sauce
- 1 cup sugar
- 1 cup vinegar
- 5 cup water
- 1 tbsp minced garlic
- 1 tbsp minced chilli

Fresh greens: Lettuce, mints, perilla, cilantro, etc
2   kg rice vermicelli noodle
2. Instruction

Grilled meat

There are two types of grilled meat in the traditional Bun Cha: grilled pork patties and grilled pork slices. Grilled pork patties are made from minced shoulder pork and grilled pork slices are made from thinly sliced pork belly.

Marinate both types of meat with salt, fish sauce, oyster sauce, sugar, minced shallots and garlic and pepper. Set aside for at least 2 hours for the better flavor absorption (Preferably, leave it sit overnight (if for lunch) or leave it from the morning (if for dinner) in the refrigerator.

After that, grill the sliced pork and pork patties outdoor on charcoal until both sides are golden brown. Oven is can also be the alternation for charcoal with the ideal temperature being 190 – 200 degree C. Don't forget to cover a thin layer of oil over the meat to prevent drying out during being grilled.

Pickles

To make pickles, slice green papaya and carrots thinly into flower shape. Kohlrabi and cucumber are also substitutes for green papaya. Mix them with 2 tsp salt. After 5 minutes, rinse them well and slightly squeeze out the excess water. Next, add the mixture with sugar and vinegar (or lime juice). Set aside for 30 minutes for the veggies can absorb the flavor.

Dipping sauce

Dipping sauce is the soul of Bun Cha and many other Vietnamese cuisines. To make dipping sauce, dissolve sugar and vinegar in fish sauce and water in a sauce pan over medium low heat. The golden ratio for making Bun Cha dipping sauce is 1 sugar: 1 fish sauce: 1 vinegar: 5water. Minced garlic and chili should be added to add more intense flavor for the sauce.

Boil the rice vermicelli

With fresh rice vermicelli, just quickly poach it through hot water before serving so that the rice vermicelli noodle can be soften and soak up the dipping sauce better.

With dried rice vermicelli, soak the dried one into warm water until it is soften. After that, boil it into a pot of hot water. Transfer the hot boiled rice vermicelli into a colander, rinse it under the cold water in 30 – 45 seconds and drain it to prevent it sticky together.

Assemble the dish

To assemble the dish, fill a bowl with warm dipping sauce and pickles. Then add some grilled sliced pork and pork patties. Place the fresh greens in one dish and the noodles into another dish. To serve, dip the some of the noodles into the sauce and eat with grilled meat and herbs.

2. Pho bo (Beef pho or Beef noodle soup)

Pho is practically the national dish of Vietnam. In Vietnam, beef pho is a classic and is seen to be a comfort dish that can eat anytime of a day.

Pho is also well-known around the world due to its natural savory broth, chewy noodles, the tenderness of the beef slices and the spicy and herby garnishes on top.

1. Ingredients (6 servings)

- 5 pounds knuckle bones
- 2 pounds beef chuck (half for cooked meat, half for medium rare meat)
- Raw beef
- 2 gingers
- 2 onions
- 10 star anise
- 5 black cardamom
- 2-4cm cinnamon sticks
- 5 shallots
- 2 kg noodles

- Fish sauce

- Bean sprouts

2. Instruction

Char and slightly boil beef bones

Charred beef bones. Add charred beef bones and a half of beef chuck to a pot of water and bring it to a boil on high heat. Cook for 5 minutes or until all the impurities rise to the top. Wash bones and meat carefully. (This will help make the broth clear). Discard the water in which the meat cooked. (This cleans the bones and meat and reduces the impurities that can cloud the broth.)

Char gingers, onions, shallots, cinnamon sticks, star anises and black cardamom

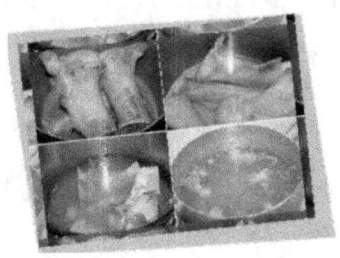

Char all of gingers, onions, shallots, cinnamon sticks, star anises and black cardamom until fragrant. You do not have to blacken entire surface, just enough to make them slightly soften and bring out the aroma. Use tongs to occasionally rotate them and to grab and discard any flyaway shallots skin. After charring, use sharp knife to remove their burned skin and wash off their blackened bits (if any). With gingers and shallots, don't forget to mash the gingers and shallots so that their inner juice can be released.

Tie all charred gingered, shallots, cinnamon sticks, star anises and black cardamom in a piece of cheesecloth for dropping it in the broth.

Cook the broth and beef chuck

Add all of the washed charred boiled beef bones, beef chuck and the piece of charred gingered, shallots, cinnamon sticks, star anises, black cardamom into a large stockpot of water. When the water returns to a boil, reduce the heat to a simmer. Skim the surface often to remove any foam and fat.

Simmer until the beef chuck is tender (about 1-2 hours). Take it out of the broth and submerge it in cool water to prevent the meat from darkening and drying out. Drain, then cut into paper thin slices and set aside. Regarding the broth, season the broth with salt, sugar, and fish sauce. Continue simmering the broth until you're ready to assemble the dish.

Slightly boil noodles

With fresh noodles, just quickly poach it through hot water before serving so that the noodles can be soften and prevent them cooling down the broth

Assemble the dish

To serve, place the warm noodles in a bowl. Place a few slices of the beef chuck and the remaining raw beef on the noodles. Garnish with onion, scallions and cilantro. Pour the boiling broth into each bowl. Serve immediately. You can add bean sprouts, herbs, chilies, lime juice and black pepper to have more intense for the dish.

3. Banh Da Cua (Red Noodle Soup With Crab)

Red noodle soup with crab is seen to be a delicacy of the port – Hai phong city of Vietnam. One of the key ingredients to make this dish special is the red flat noodles. They are made from rice. The rice is well drain and soaked into water for hours. The soaked rice was masticated and diluted to become a liquid. Then people girdle and bake it to make the special red rice noodles.

The food is very eye-catchy of the red noodles, red tomatoes and chilli, green vegetable, pink brown of the crab, navy of betel rolls and yellow dried shallots. Needless to say, the flavor is unique and amazing that no one can deny.

1. Ingredients (3-4 servings)

- 2 packs of Banh Da Do flat noodles (Red flat noodles)
- 500g minced crab
- 300g pork rib

- 150g minced pork shoulder
- ½ tsp shrimp paste
- 2 tomatoes
- 2 Packs of betel leaves
- A handful of wood ear mushrooms
- Morning glory
- Shallots
- Green onions
- Cilantro
- Perilla
- Bean sprouts
- Lettuce

2. Instruction

Make the pork broth
Wash the pork rib. Cut in pieces. Par boil the rib pieces in boiling water in 5 minutes and drain. Wash again the parboiled rib pieces and add them to another large pot and bring to a boil. Simmer on a low heat for 2 hours to make the broth.

Make the crab broth
Slowly add water to minced crab and gently squeeze. Wait for a while until the crab residue subsides. The remaining crab water is used to make crab broth. Low heat the crab broth, season with salt and ½ tsp fish sauce, gently stir in order to make the crab-roe flows onto the broth surface. Take the crab-roe out and set aside. Pour the remaining precooked crab broth into the boiling pork rib broth.

On another pot, stir fry the sliced tomatoes, thinly sliced shallots. Add ¼ tsp salt.

In the large pot of mixture of crab broth and pork rib broth, add the combination of stir-fried tomatoes and shallots and crab-roe. Simmer on a low-heat.

Make the spring rolls with betel leaves

Mix the minced pork with thinly sliced wood ear mushrooms and chopped green onions together, season with salt and pepper.

Put 1 spoon of meat mixture onto a betel leave. Roll it up to make a roll. Do the same with the remaining and fry them on a non-stick skillet.

Parboil morning glory and Banh Da Do flat noodle

Wash morning glory. Cut in pieces and quickly parboil in order to keep it crispy.

Banh Da Do flat noodles are par-boiled until they are soften.

Assemble the dish

Add pre-boiled noodles to a bowl. Place a few of betel spring rolls, cooked pork ribs, crab-row on the noodles. Garnish with parboiled morning glory, chopped green onions, and green herbs (coriander, perilla, lettuce, bean sprouts) and ladle the steaming hot broth into the bowl.

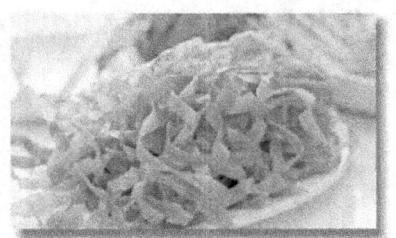

4. Nem Ran (Vietnamese Fried Spring Rolls)

Vietnamese fried spring rolls are a traditional dish of Vietnam. The dish is call "Nem ran" in northern Vietnam and "Cha gio" in southern Vietnam. They often appear on special occasions of the year such as New year, Tet and other family festivities. But today, they can be served all year around and present in almost every menu of Vietnamese restaurants for foreigners.

In foreign tourists' eyes, the dish has delicate flavor: crunchy and chewy with a bubbly surface and is combined with sweet and sour dipping sauce but is still balanced with green herbs.

Spring rolls have many recipes and variants such as Crab spring rolls, seafood spring rolls, and mushroom spring rolls. But traditional classic spring rolls are still at every Vietnamese's heart. They are often served with Bun Cha.

1. Ingredients (20 rolls for 5-6 servings)

- 200g minced pork
- 200g minced shrimp
- 2 carrots
- 5 dried wood ear mushrooms
- 50g glass noodles
- 1 egg
- 20-24 dried round rice paper wrappers (Bánh tráng)
- 50g bean sprouts
- Scallions
- 1 handful mint leaves
- 1 handful coriander
- 1 handful perilla leaves

2. **Instruction**

Slice the ingredients
Soak the dried wood ear mush rooms and dried glass noodles in warm water for 15 minutes until they are soften. Then wash off. Slice thinly the wood ear mush rooms.

Slice thinly carrots.

Chop sliced wood ear mushrooms, carrots, bean sprouts and soft glass noodles in small pieces (about 3 cm)

Chop scallions in small pieces (0.5 cm)
Mix the ingredients

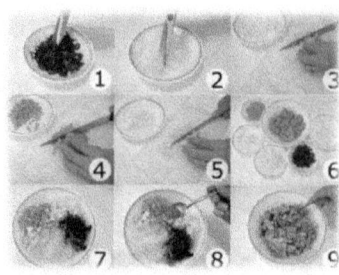

Add mince pork, minced shrimps, sliced and chopped ingredients into a big bowl. Add 1 egg to help ingredients adhere together. Mix well and leave it sit for about 15 minutes. You can add black pepper but don't add salt into the mixture because it will make the rolls more salty since the wrappers have their seasoning themselves and we have dipping sauce to add strong flavor for the rolls.

Wrap And Fry The Rolls

Prepare a large flat tray with 1cm of water into which you should quickly submerge one sheet of rice paper, for no more than a second, then quickly lay it on your work surface.

Place 1 tablespoon of filling mixture into the center of a softened rice paper sheet. Fold the bottom edge into the center, covering the filling. Fold in opposing edges and roll up tightly. Repeat with remaining rice paper wrappers.

Fry the spring rolls in batches of 3 or 4 until crisp and golden brown on both sides, about 5 minutes. Drain off the excess oil on oil absorbing cooking paper.

Assemble the dish

To serve, place the spring rolls (in whole or cut in halves) on a tray with mounds of fresh greens and herbs; and a small bowl of dipping sauce. Fried spring rolls are also accompanied with Bun Cha.

5. "Nem Thinh" (Pig Ears And Meat Coated With Powdered Grill Rice)

"Nem Thinh" (Pig ears and meat coated with powdered grill rice) originated from Nam Dinh province and is now a popular dish in Northern cities of Vietnam. The dish is best eaten in summer and is often served with drinking beers. Its crunchy and chewy of the pig ears and meet go harmony with the green veggies and sour sweet dipping sauce will make you never forget this dish.

1. Ingredients (4-5 servings)

- 300g Pig ears
- 100g Pork lean meat
- 200g Powdered grill rice
- 3-4 Lime leaves
- Chopped garlic
- Chopped chili
- Fish sauce

- Lime juice
- Sugar
- Pepper
- Vinegar
- A handful of cluster fig leaves
- A handful of polyscias fruticosa leaves

Ingredients for "Nem Thinh"
(Pig ears and meat coated with powdered grill rice)

2. Instruction

Shave the pig ears carefully. Wash pig ears and lean pork with little salt.

Prepare a pot and fill with water. Add pig ear and lean pork into the pot and bring to a boil for 20 minutes. When they are cooked, put them into cold water for a couple minutes to prevent the meat darken. Drain and slice thinly to pieces and set aside.

Powdered grilled rice

Lime leaves are sliced super thinly. Mash garlic and chopped. Chili is chopped.

Add salt, pepper to the plate of sliced pork ear and meat.

Then add powdered grilled rice to the mixture. Squeeze well. Finally, add sliced lime leaves, chopped garlic and chopped chili to the mixture.

To make the dipping sauce, remember the golden rule: 4 fish sauce: 2 water: 1 lime juice: 1 sugar: ½ pepper: 1 vinegar and chopped garlic and chopped chilli.

Assemble the dish

To serve, pork ears and meat are rolled by cluster fig leaves and dip in the dipping sauce. To add more intense flavor, serve the dish with green herbs such as polyscias fruticosa leaves.

6. Sua Dau Nanh (Soy Milk)

Soy milk has become a popular mainstream drink in Vietnam. You can find it in every corner , especially instant packed soy milk are sold in every convenient stores. The more premium version is found on organic store or healthy organic soy-based chains.

Soy milk is very healthy for bodies. It provides B-complex vitamins, Calcium and Iron. In Vietnam, soy milk is served as a breakfast drink to boost energy. It is also consumed widely as a dessert drink.

1. Ingredients (2liters serving)

- 1.5 cup organic soy beans
- 8 cups water
- 0.25 cup sugar
- 6-8 Pandan leaves

2. Instruction

Clean soy beans
Put the soy beans into a large bowl and rinse few times until the water is clear.

Soak the beans in a cold water overnight or at least 8 hours. They will expand a little bit. Rinse beans one more time and drain.

Blend beans

Pour the beans into a blender and add enough water to cover the beans. Turn on the blender at maximum speed until smoothly blended.
Pour the blended soy milk into a piece of cheesecloth. Firmly squeeze the cloth to extract the soy milk. Continue until all that is left is the pulp. Pour the soy milk into a large saucepan.
Pandan leaves in soy milk
Heat the milk over Medium Low heat. Skim the foam from the top and discard. Stir the milk every few minutes to keep it from burning. When it comes to a gentle boil, reduce the heat and simmer on Low for 10 minutes.

Add the sugar and pandan leaves and stir until the sugar is dissolved. Continue cooking on low heat for another 10 minutes.

Turn-off the heat and allow the milk to cool for 15 minutes.

Strain the soy milk and skim off the foam again.

Serve the soy milk hot or cold.

7. Banh Xeo Mien Tay (Vietnamese Sizzling Crepe)

Banh xeo is a savory crepe that is pan-fried and generously topped with pork belly, shrimps, bean sprouts and other green veggies. "Xeo" in Banh xeo refers to the sizzling sound when the batter is cooked. In most of southern Vietnam and Saigon, Banh xeo mien Tay (South-western) is a crowd-pleaser with its rich taste due to the liberal use of coconut milk. This style is also universally accepted abroad as the flamboyant mascot of Banh Xeo.

Its crispy flavor balanced with green herbs will crave you to make and eat it often.

Ingredients (4 – 5 servings)

For Banh xeo:

- (400g) 1 bag of Banh xeo flour
- 250ml Coconut milk
- 1 tsp ground turmeric
- Olive oil

- 0.5kg raw medium shrimp
- 0.3kg pork belly
- 0.2 kg bean sprouts
- Chopped green onions
- Chopped coriander

For dipping sauce:

- Sugar
- Fish sauce
- Lime juice
- Chopped garlic
- Chopped chilli

1. Instruction

Mix the batter

Whisk the flour together with coconut milk, chopped green onion, salt, ground turmeric and 1/4 cup cold water in a bowl until completely smooth. Set aside.
Cook the filling

Wash the shrimps and pork belly. Cut pork belly into thin slices.

Prepare a non-stick skillet over a medium high heat with oil. Add shrimps and pork belly slices and season with chopped shallots, salt, and pepper. Once shrimps and meat are cooked, add bean sprouts to the skillet to cook. Set aside. Don't cook too long; otherwise, beansprouts won't keep crispy.

Make the crepe

Add ¼ cup of batter to the skillet. Quickly tilt and swirl batter around until the bottom of the pan is coated with a thin layer.

Add the pre-cooked filling onto the half of the crepe. Sprinkle with chopped corianders and mints.

Slide crepe onto plate and flip it so it folds over the filling and leave it on the pan until both sides go yellow and become crispy.

Dipping sauce

To make the dipping sauce for Banh xeo, remember the ratio 5 water: 2 sugar: 1.5 fish sauce: 1 lime juice. And add more chopped garlic and chilli into the sauce for have more intense flavor and stunning visual.

Assemble the dish

To serve, wrap Banh xeo with green spinach or rice paper, accompanied by green herbs such as cilantro, perilla and basil. Cut Banh xeo in pieces and dip in the dipping sauce.

8. Xoi Vo (Sweet Rice Coated With Mung Beans)

Among all types of sticky rice in Vietnam, Xoi vo (sweet rice coated with mung beans) is not only often served in specially occasions in Vietnam such as Tet, New year and other family festivities, but it is also used as a dessert for elders and children because of its sweetness and easy to combine with sweet pudding.

1. Ingredients(4-5 servings)

- 1 cup peeled mung beans
- 2 cup glutinous rice
- Salt
- Oil
- Sugar

2. Instruction

Wash and soak the glutinous rice and yellow mung beans separately in warm water for at least 8 hours (preferably overnight).

After soaking, wash again, drain them and set apart.

Add ½ tsp salt to the bean and steam for 20 minutes until well cooked. It's easy to mash the well cook beans in your fingers to check the cooked condition of the beans. Set aside to let cool.

Use a blender to ground the bean until becoming powders. Divide cooked bean powder into two portions.

First portion: is mixed with glutinous rice. Add 2 tsp oil, ½ tsp salt to the mixture and steam over a medium heat until cooked for about 30 minutes. Pour the cooked rice on a plate and set aside.

Second portion: is mixed with the cooked rice. Add 2 tsp sugar to the mixture. Stir well and steam the mixture one more time in 10 minutes. Transfer the rice to a plate and serve hot or cool.

Assemble the dish

Sticky rice coated with mung beans is served hot or cool with sweet dessert as mung bean pudding.

9. Cha Ca La Vong (La Vong Grilled Turmeric Fish With Dill)

Cha Ca La Vong (La Vong grilled turmeric fish with dill) is a delicious and iconic dish of Hanoi. Besides Pho, Cha ca La Vong represents the elegance and complexity of Hanoi cuisine. At it's originating roots from the 100+ year old Chả Cá Lã Vọng restaurant, turmeric marinaded fish is first grilled and then fried table-side. It's served with tons of fresh dill, other herbs, crush peanuts, and rice noodles. The dish looks stunning with golden fish and green herbs. Its flavor is an amazing combination of sweet, salty, sour and umami. If you visit Hanoi, Cha Ca La Vong is a must-try.

1. Ingredients (4 servings)

- 1 kg Hemibagrus fillets (Cá lăng) or Tilapia or Catfish
- 1 Fresh galangal
- 1 Fresh turmeric
- ¼ tsp shrimp paste
- ½ tsp sugar

- ½ tsp mẻ (or lemon juice as a substitute)
- 1 tsp fish sauce
- 1 kg rice vermicelli noodles
- 100g peanuts
- 1 bunch fresh dill
- 1 bunch green onions
- Olive oil

2. Instruction

Prepare the fish

Clean the fish and drain. Cut the fillets into 1.5cm pieces. Set aside.
Put on a pair of gloves or plastic bags to avoid turmeric stains. Peel off the skins of galangal and turmeric. Cut them into thin slices. Pound slices with a pestle to release the juice. Set aside.

Marinade

Marinate the fish with galangal and turmeric juice, shrimp paste, fish sauce, sugar and "mẻ" and leave them sit for 1 hour. After that, grill the seasoned fish on charcoal until both sides go yellow.

 Assemble the dish

To serve, prepare a cast-iron skillet over a medium high heat with a bit of olive oil on the bottom. Fry the pre-grilled fish. Add a bit of dill and green onions to the oil for a quick sear. Prepare a bowl of rice vermicelli noodles. Transfer cooked fish and dill to the noodles. Add a ladle of shrimp paste and top with peanuts.

10. Goi Cuon (Vietnamese Fresh Summer Rolls)

Goi cuon (Vietnamese fresh summer rolls) is a refreshing appetizer made up of shrimp, pork, vermicelli noodles, and an assortment of vegetables rolled in rice paper. The dish is best eaten in summer due to its healthy recipe, fresh flavor and the availableness of the green veggies.

1. Ingredients (6 servings)

For the rolls

- 0.5 kg pork shoulder or pork belly
- 0.5 kg shrimps
- 1 bag of 200gr rice vermicelli noodles (bún in Vietnamese)
- Beansprouts

- Carrots (sliced thinly)
- 2-3 Cucumber (splitted in half and sliced at an angle)
- Lettuce, mint, basil, perillla (washed and dried)

For dipping sauce

- 1 tablespoon soy sauce
- 1.5 tsp peanut butter
- 1 sugar
- 1-2 tablespoon hot water
- 1 tsp chili oil
- Sesame seeds (optional)

2. Instruction

Prepare the ingredients

Bring a large pot of water to a boil. Put the pork shoulder/pork belly in the boiling water until it's cooked (about 30-45 minutes). Soak the boiled pork under cold water for 15 minutes to prevent the meat darken. Slice thinly the meat and set aside.

In the same pot of boiling water, put the shrimp in and cook until it's pink. Take them out and put them into the water ice bath to cool. Peel the skin and slit the shrimp in half, lengthwise. Set aside

If you have fresh rice vermicelli noodles, just poach it quickly over warm water to make it soften. If you have dried rice vermicelli noodles, bring it to a boil until it's cooked and become soften.

Wrap the rolls

Quickly dip the rice paper in some water to make it become soften.

Place the softened rice paper onto a clean plate.

First, add some lettuce, mint, basil and perilla on the rice paper. Then add pork, shrimp, noodles and cucumber on top. Fold in the sides, then roll it up. Repeat with the remaining. Serve immediately with dipping sauce.

Dipping sauce

To make the dipping sauce, just combine all of the ingredients and stir well. Adjust seasoning to taste.

Part 2

Recipes Different Types Of Vietnamese Dipping Sauces

Basic Recipes

Viet-Style Stocks

Nước dùng

Stocks are used as a liquid base for soups, congees, stir-fries, and sauces. Vietnamese stocks are quite different from western-style stocks due to the difference in herbs and aromatics that are used.

Non-vegetarian Vietnamese Stocks

Nước dùng mặn

- 1kg: Bones, chicken or pork, rinsed well
- 12 cups: Water
- 1 tsp: White peppercorns
- 5-6 cloves: Shallots
- ½: Onion, wedged
- 1: Ginger, small size, smashed
- ½ tsp: Salt

In a large stockpot, add bones, cover with cold water, and bring to a boil over high heat. Once pot is boiling, skim off any foam and fat that has floated to the surface. Reduce the heat to low and simmer for about 1 to 2 hours.

When finished, strain and set aside to cool. The stock is now ready for use.

Vegetarian Stock

Nước dùng chay

- 12 cups: Water
- 1: Daikon Radish, medium size, peeled, sliced into big chunks
- 1: Carrot, big size, peeled, sliced into big chunks
- 1: Chayote, big size, peeled, largely diced
- ½ tsp: Salt
- ½ tsp: White peppercorns

In a large stockpot, add all the ingredients, cover with water and bring to a boil over high heat. Once pot is boiling, skim off any foam that has floated to the surface. Reduce the heat to low and simmer for about 1 hour.

When finished, strain and set aside to cool. The stock is now ready for use.

Annatto Oil

Dầu mầu điều

- 1Tbsp: Annatto Seeds
- 2Tbsp: Cooking Oil

Heat a skillet, add oil and annatto seeds. Let it fry for about 5-6 minutes over medium heat or until the oil turns a reddish color. Remove from heat and let it cool off completely. Strain and discard seeds and set aside to cool. Pour into a glass container.

Pickled Kohlrabi And Carrot

Dưa góp Su hào và Cà rốt

- 1: Kohlrabi
- 1: Carrot
- ½ tsp: Salt
- 2Tbsp: Sugar
- 3Tbsp: Vinegar
- 2 cloves: Garlic, minced
- 1: Chili Pepper, sliced

Peel the Kohlrabi and Carrot then julienne. Rub with salt and set aside for about 10 minutes, then rinse well with boiling water. Squeeze out as much extra water as possible and put the vegetables in a big bowl. Add sugar and vinegar, and toss to mix well. Let sit for about 1 hour. Finally, add minced garlic and chili pepper. Pickled vegetables now are ready to serve.

Pickled Carrot And Daikon Radish

Dưa góp Cà rốt và Củ cải

- 1: Daikon Radish, small size
- 1: Carrot, medium size
- 1 tsp: Salt
- 5Tbsp: Vinegar
- 5Tbsp: Sugar
- 1 cup: Water

Peel carrot and daikon, wash clean, then julienne into 5cm long thin strips.

Rub vegetables with salt and let them rest for about 10 minutes. Then rinse well under running water. Remove from the water, and squeeze out as much water as possible.

Combine vinegar, sugar and water in a big jar. Stir well until sugar is completely dissolved. Place carrot and daikon radish in the jar. Let soak for about one day until done.

Dipping Sauces (Most Popular)
- Nước chấm

Dipping sauces reflect the delicacy of Vietnamese cuisine. They are very diverse and they become an integral part of our daily meals. There are 12 popular types of dipping sauces:

Dipping Sauce For Barbecue Meat
Nước chấm thịt nướng

Yields: about 1/2 cup
Preparation Time: 15 minutes
Cooking Time: 10 minutes
Tricks: You can make the sauce in advance and keep it in the fridge, but leave the papaya and carrot out until the time of serving.

- 5 Tbsp: Water
- 1 Tbsp: Vinegar
- 1 Tbsp: Honey or granulated sugar
- 1 Tbsp: Fish Sauce
- ½ tsp: Ground Pepper
- 2 Tbsp: Green Papaya, peeled, finely sliced, salted then rinsed well, dried
- 2 Tbsp: Carrot, peeled, finely sliced, salted then rinsed well, dried

In a small pot, stir water, vinegar, honey or sugar, fish sauce, and ground pepper. Bring to a simmer over medium heat, and let simmer for about 3-4 minutes until the sugar/honey is completely dissolved. In a medium sized bowl, mix with sliced papaya and carrot. Add more ground pepper to taste. Serve warm.

Dipping Sauce For Spring Rolls Or Fried Foods
Nước chấm nem rán và đồ chiên rán

Method 1 (runny liquid)

Amount: about 2/3 cup
Preparation time: 10 minutes
Tricks: Similar to the sauce for Barbecue Meat, this sauce contains more chopped garlic and chili pepper for a stronger flavor.
- 3 gloves: Garlic
- 1: Chili pepper
- ¼ Tbsp: Ground Pepper
- 9-10 Tbsp: Water
- 2 Tbsp: Fish Sauce
- 2 Tbsp: Sugar, granulated
- 1 Tbsp: Vinegar
- 1 Tbsp: Lime Juice
- 2 Tbsp: Green Papaya, peeled, finely sliced, salted then rinsed well, dried
- 2 Tbsp: Carrot, peeled, finely sliced, salted then rinsed well, dried

Method 2 (thicker liquid)

Amount: about 2/3 cup

Preparation time: 10 minutes
Tricks: This dipping sauce can be made days before serving and kept in the fridge.
- 1: Spur Chili, minced
- 1 clove: Garlic, minced
- 4Tbsp: Sugar, granulated
- 4Tbsp: Vinegar
- a pinch: Salt
- 2-3Tbsp: Water
- 1Tbsp: Peanut, roasted, crushed (optional)

Mix spur chili, garlic, sugar, vinegar together, then bring to a boil over a medium heat. Add water and stir well. Reduce the mixture until it has thickened to a sauce, and remove from heat.

Transfer sweet chili sauce to a serving bowl, and drizzle crushed peanut on top. Ready to serve.

Dipping Sauce For Seafood

Nước chấm (đồ ăn) Hải sản

Nước chấm = Dipping sauce; Hải sản = Seafood; Đồ ăn: dishes

This sort of dipping sauce helps reduce the pungent aroma of seafood.

Served primarily in the home, this sauce is rarely seen in big restaurants, where the chefs have their own individual methods for making seafood dips.

Amount: ½ cup
Preparation Time: 5 minutes

Cooking Time: 5 minutes

Tricks: You can make this 1 day in advance and store in the fridge, but for freshest flavour, make the dip the day it is served. Using Mint brings the best flavour for the dip.

- 1: Chili pepper, smashed
- 3-4 gloves: Garlic, minced
- 1 ½ Tbsp: Honey or sugar
- 1 Tbsp: Coriander stems, minced
- 1 Tbsp: Mint, minced
- 2 Tbsp: Fish Sauce
- 3 Tbsp: Lime Juice

Combine all ingredients into a bowl, and stir to mix.

Taste and adjust the seasoning: the flavour should lead with sour, followed by salty, and finally the sweetness should be the lightest. The sugar serves only to cut the saltiness and balance the acid.

Dipping Sauce For Summer Roll

Nước chấm gỏi cuốn

Nước chấm = Dipping sauce; Gỏi cuốn= Summer Roll

There are different dips for summer rolls. This is caused by the regional variations. In the south of Vietnam, the dish is made with peanut sauce, peanut with hoisin sauce or anchovy paste. Meanwhile, In the north of Vietnam, it is more like a sweet and sour dip like I have introduced previously as dipping sauce for spring rolls or barbecue meat.

Peanut+Hoisin Sauce

Nước chấm tương đậu phộng
Yields: 1 cup
Preparation Time: 15 minutes
Cooking Time: 15 minutes
Tricks: You can make this sauce in advance and keep it in a fridge 1 day before serving but leave the peanut out until the time of serving.

- 1 tsp: Cooking Oil
- 1 tsp: Garlic, minced
- 3 Tbsp: Hoisin sauce
- 5 Tbsp: Chicken or pork broth
- 1.5 Tbsp: Peanut Butter
- 1Tbsp: Tamarind juice
- 1 tsp: Honey
- 1 tsp: Chili Pepper, minced
- 1 tsp: Roasted Peanuts, crushed

Heat cooking oil in a small saucepan over medium heat. Fry minced garlic until it begins to yellow. Add hoisin sauce, broth, and peanut butter. Stir well then add tamarind sauce and honey. Stir again and simmer on low heat for 1-2 minutes, uncovered, until slightly thickened. Pour the sauce into condiment bowls and top with minced fresh chili and crushed peanuts. It is ready to serve.

Anchovy Sauce

Mắm nêm

Yields: 1 cup
Preparation Time: 15-20 minutes
Cooking Time: 15 minutes
Notes: Do not bring the sauce to a boiling point. As this will dilute the smell of the fermented anchovy sauce, the star of the dish.

- 1-2 cloves: Garlic, minced
- 1tsp: Lemongrass, minced
- 1tsp: Sugar
- 2tsp: Vinegar
- 2tsp: Pineapple, crushed
- 2Tbsp: Fermented Anchovy Sauce
- ½ cup: Chicken Broth
- 1: Chili Pepper, minced
- ¼ tsp: Ground Pepper
- 1Tbsp: Vegetable Oil

Heat vegetable oil in a pot and fry minced garlic and lemongrass until it becomes a golden brown. Add pineapple and chili pepper. Stir well, and reduce the heat to medium low and simmer for just 30 seconds. Add chicken stock and anchovy sauce. Add sugar and vinegar. Stir well until sugar completely dissolved. Remove from the heat. Transfer to a serving bowl.

For serving:
Summer Roll
Grilled Fish
Rice vermicelli in Fermented Fish Soup
Grilled Beef wrapped in Betel leaves

Tamarind Fish Sauce

Nước mắm me
Yields: 1 cup
Preparation Time: 10-15 minutes
Cooking Time: 15 minutes
Notes: You can make this 1-2 days in advance and store in the fridge in a tightly sealed jar.

- 3 Tbsp: Tamarind juice
- 2 Tbsp: Fish Sauce
- 3 Tbsp: Coconut Sugar
- 3 Tbsp: Chicken Broth
- 1 Tbsp: Vegetable Oil
- 1 tsp: Garlic, minced

Heat the oil in a small pot, fry minced garlic until it becomes a golden brown. Add chicken broth and sugar. Stir well until sugar is fully dissolved. Add tamarind juice and fish sauce. Mix well. Remove from the heat and transfer to a cup to serve.

For serving:
Seafood, boiled, steamed, pan-fried or grilled
Rice Paper Salad
Dressing Sauce for Mixing Pho

Dipping Sauce For Dumplings

Nước chấm bánh hấp

Yields: ½ cup

Preparation time: 3 minutes

Tricks: The sauce can be made in advance and kept in the fridge for a few days before serving

- 2 Tbsp: Soy Sauce
- 2 Tbsp: Vinegar
- 1 tsp: Dark/black Soy Sauce
- 1: Chili pepper, finely chopped
- 1 tsp: Sugar, granulated

Combine all the ingredients in a bowl. Mix well until sugar is fully dissolved. Sauce is ready to serve.

Dipping Sauce For Steamed Rolled Rice Pancake

Nước chấm Bánh Cuốn

Nước chấm = Dipping Sauce, Bánh Cuốn = Steamed Rolled Rice Pancake

Yields: 2 cups

Preparation time: 20 minutes

Tricks: You can make the sauce in advance, but the lime juice is only squeezed in at the time of serving.

- 2 cups: Water
- 1tsp: Sugar, granulated
- 1tsp: Hot water
- 2Tbsp: Fish Sauce
- 1-2: Chili Pepper, finely chopped
- 3-4 cloves: Garlic, crushed

- 1tsp: Ground Pepper
- 1: Lemon, cut into small pieces or wedges, set aside.

Add sugar to hot water and mix well until sugar is fully dissolved. Add water, fish sauce, garlic, and chili. Stir well. Drizzle with ground pepper.

Dipping Sauce For Pancako

Nước chấm Bánh Xèo

Yield: 1 cup

Preparation time: 10 minutes

Tricks: The sauce can be made in advance and stored in the fridge, but do not add the vegetables until serving time.

- ½ Tbsp: Rice Vinegar
- 1Tbsp: Honey or Sugar
- ½ Tbsp: Lime Juice
- 1Tbsp: Fish Sauce
- 5Tbsp: Water
- 2-3 cloves: Garlic, minced
- 1: Chili Pepper, finely chopped
- ¼ cup: Pickled Daikon and Carrot; **recipe in page 71**

Combine vinegar with honey/sugar, lime juice, fish sauce and water in a bowl. Mix well until honey/sugar is fully dissolved. Add pickled vegetables, and top with minced garlic and chopped chili pepper.

Vegetables Dips

Kho quẹt

This is the specialty of people in the west of Vietnam. The dip tastes salty, followed with sweeteness and a hint of firekick.

Yields: 1 cup

Preparation Time: 15 minutes

Cooking Time: 20 minutes

Tricks: Use a small to medium size of dried shrimp to have the best result as the shrimp is tender and sweet. Kho quẹt can be made in advance and stored in the fridge for a few days before serving.

FOR THE DIP
- 1 cup: Fish Sauce
- ¼ cup: Water
- 1 cup: Pork Belly, finely sliced
- ½ cup: Dried Shrimp, soaked in hot water, rinsed well
- 3-4Tbsp: Sugar
- 2 Tbsp: Shallot, minced

FOR GARNISH
- 2-3: Chili Pepper, smashed
- 2 Tbps: Green Onion, finely chopped
- ½ tsp: Ground Pepper

Heat a skillet over medium high heat. Add pork belly, and fry for about 10 minutes or until the fat separates. Remove the pork from the fat and set it aside.

Bring the skillet containing the fat back to heat, add minced shallot, keep stirring until it turns golden brown. Pour in fish sauce, then add sugar and water. Mix to stir and let it cook until the sugar fully dissolved. Add shrimp, mix well. Add pork belly. Let it simmer for about 8-10 minutes over low heat until the water reduces to a thick sauce consistency. Add smashed chili pepper on top. Remove from heat.

To assemble: Transfer the mixture to a serving bowl, sprinkle chopped green onion and ground pepper on top. Serve at room temperature or warm.

For serving:
Boiled vegetables
Cooked rice

Vegetarian Dipping Sauce

Nước chấm chay

Yields: ½ cup

Preparation Time: 10 minutes

Tricks: You can make the sauce in advance and keep it in the fridge the day before serving.

- 3Tbsp: Soy Sauce
- 2Tbsp: Sugar
- 1Tbsp: Lime
- 2Tbsp: Water
- 1: Chili Pepper, finely chopped

Combine all the ingredients in a bowl. Mix well until sugar is fully dissolved.

For serving:
Stir-fry Vegetables with Noodles
Steamed vegetarian cakes

Noodles & Glass Noodles

Bún/Phở/Miến

'Pho' Noodles Soup

Phở

Phở = pho noodles soup

Pho noodles is considered to national dish of Vietnam. It has been one of the most popular street foods since the day it originated in the early 20th century. There are several styles of Pho that are served, such as Hanoi style and Saigon style. Each style differs by the width of noodles, sweetness of broth, and choice of herbs. There are many varieties of Pho. Namely, stir-fried pho - phở xào, sautéed pho - phở áp chảo, wrapped&rolled pho - phở cuốn, and sour pho - phở chua.

Some similarity they all share, however, are broth which is made from animal bones (particularly chicken and beef) and spices, which usually include star anise, coriander seeds, coriander roots, cinnamon, cardamom, ginger, shallot. If you walk in any Pho restaurants, whether in Vietnam or abroad, you can see the common side-table condiments including fish sauce, seasoning powder, sriracha sauce, garlic and chili pepper pickles, hoisin sauce and ground pepper. Pho has won the heart of not only Vietnamese people, but also people around the world with its super aromatic, clear, and nutritious soup.

Beef Noodles Soup

Phở Bò

Serve: 4-5

Preparation Time: 30 minutes

Cooking Time: 2 hours

Tricks: Do not drop the spices into the stock pot at the beginning as the flavor will be reduced when cooked.

THE MIXTURE OF SPICES
- ½ Tbsp: Salt
- 1Tbsp: Seasoning powder
- 1 ½ Tbsp: Sugar, rock

THE HERBS
- 3: Star Anise
- 3: Cinnamon
- 3-4: Cardamom
- 4-5 cloves: Shallot, smashed
- 1: Ginger, medium size, smashed
- 4-5: Coriander Roots

FOR GARNISH
- 2: Lime, wedged

- 2: Chilli Pepper, finely cut
- 1: Onion, cut into fine slices
- a handful: Sawtooth, finely cut
- a handful: Coriander, finely cut
- a handful: Green Onion, green part: finely cut; white part: cut into thin strips

THE REST
- 400g: Pho Noodles
- 200g: Beef, sirloin or tenderloin
- 500g: Beef Bones, chopped into 5-6cm length
- 800g: Beef Brisket

Soak the noodles in room-temperature water for about 1 hour until the noodles turn white and are pliable. Remove from water and set aside.

Cut sirloin or tenderloin into very thin slices. Set aside.

Toast star anise, cinnamon and cardamom in a frying pan for about 2 minutes until their flavours spead out and they turn brown.

Place shallot and ginger on a baking sheet and roast over open flame stove for about 1 minute until they blacken. Peel the shallot and discard the blackened part. Rinse again under running water. Put roasted ginger and shallot together with coriander roots and spices in a cheesebag or a tea/spicebag, and set it aside.

To make stock: Place beef bones and brisket in a large pot. Pour 8 cups water in, and bring to a boil over high heat for about 7-8 minutes. Scrap off any impurities which rise to the top. Then reduce heat to medium low and simmer for about 2 hours, stirring occasionally.

Remove from the heat and put into a bowl of cold water for about 1-2 minutes. Remove from water and let it cool. Cut brisket into thin slices, and set aside.

Bring the stock pot back to a boil. Drop the bag into the stock pot and make sure it lies submerged. Let it cook for about 20 minutes so the flavors are absorbed into the broth. Take the bag of herbs out of the pot. Add mixture of spices, and stir to mix.

Cook the noodles so they are ready to serve by dipping them in a pot of boiling water for about 40-50 seconds.

To serve, remove the noodles from the heat and transfer to a serving bowl. Place 4-5 slices of tenderloin/sirloin and brisket onto bowl of noodles. Pour the broth in the bowl. Sprinkle with a touch of chopped sawtooth, green onion, coriander onions, and ground pepper on top. Serve immediately with a wedge of lime. You can always serve with fresh vegetables of bean spouts, thai basil, coriander or sriracha and garlic-and-chili vinegar on the side.

Beef Noodle Soup

Beef Noodle Stir-Fry

Chicken Noodles Soup

Phở Gà

Phở = noodles soup; Gà means chicken

Chicken noodles soup has subtler flavor than beef noodles soup. So, the stock for the soup uses spices such as cinnamon and cardamom which do not have a strong flavor. Many cooks don't use much star anise either. In this recipe, I still use star anise as the major flavor by keeping the same amount (3) but minimizing the use of cinnamon (from 3 to 2) and eliminating the cardamom and coriander from the stock.

Aside from these differences, making Phở Gà is almost the same as making Phở Bò if you use chicken bones for broth instead of beef bones and serve with chicken meat, not beef, of course.

Grilled Pork Noodles

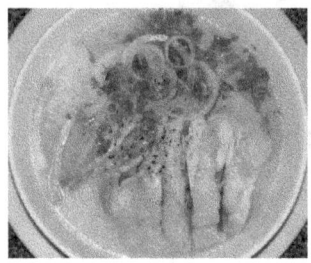

Bún Chả/Bún Thịt Nướng
Bún Chả/Bún Thịt Nướng literally means Grilled Pork Noodles. It is a type of northern Vietnamese noodle using grilled pork.
This recipe is written for two methods of cooking this dish. One is for grilling pork on charcoal, the other is for pan-searing. For both methods the result comes out similar but it depends on the weather or the tools you will have to cook this dish for picking the suitable method for you.
Serve: 3-4
Preparation Time: 20 minutes
Cooking time: 30 minutes
Special Tools: Grill (broiler) or frying pan
Tricks: Marinate the pork in the fridge for 15 minutes in advance

FOR MARINATING THE PORK
- 3 cloves: chopped shallots (medium size)
- 1 tsp: sugar
- 2tsp: chicken powder or cooking powder
- 2tsp: fish sauce
- 1 tsp: MSG
- 1 tsp: black pepper
- ½ tsp: black or dark soy sauce
- 150 gr: pork shoulder
- 150 gr: pork belly

FOR THE DRESSING
- 5Tbsp: water
- 1Tbsp: sugar
- 1Tbsp: fish sauce
- 1Tbsp: vinegar
- ¼ tsp: white pepper
- ¼ tsp: black pepper
- ½ tsp: black or dark soy sauce
- ½ cup: Mix of Green Papaya or Kohlrabi and Carrot. Thin slices.

To make dressing: Combine all the ingredients except vegetables and put them into a small pot and bring them to a boil. Toss them together until sugar dissolves completely.

Remove from the heat and stir in the green papaya (or Kohlrabi) and Carrot. Ladle into two bowls.

Finely mince the pork shoulder, then put it into one of the two bowls.

Cut pork belly into thin slices and place into the second bowl.

Combine all the seasonings for marinating the pork and divide into two parts. Put one part into each of the two bowls. Toss the pork to ensure they are evenly coated in the marinade. Marinate in the fridge for at least 15 minutes.

In a pan, add a little cooking oil and Pork belly and cook over high heat for about one minute, then turn to medium-low heat for five minutes. Flip to the other side, and repeat, turning the cooker to high heat for about one minute then turn back to medium-low heat for another five minutes. Cook until the pork become golden brown and done on both sides. Remove from the heat and put it right away to one bowl of dressing.

Clean the pan. Then, add in a little cooking oil and pork shoulder which are shaped into flattened circles. Cook over high heat first for about one minute then turn into medium-low heat for six minutes. The technique used in this period is the same as applied in the cooking Pork belly until done. Put into the second bowl.

Serve the Pork with noodles and mix of vegetables of your choice including Coleslaw, Elsholtzia, Coriando, Fish Mint, Purple Basil, Sprouts

Note: Before grilling, brush off any bits of shallots.

If using Broiler, coat the pork generously with cooking oil and grill over charcoal. Turn the pork every 2 minutes until done.

Bún thịt nướng – Grilled Pork Noodles

Mixed Pho Noodles

Phở trộn

Phở = pho noodles; Trộn is mixed

Phở trộn is literally means pho noodles are mixed with another ingredients like chicken, fresh herbs, and dipping sauce to make a complete dish. It is a modified version of traditional Pho, which is cooked and served with soup. Phở trộn is considered a dry dish. The special feature of the dish lies in the mild but well-balanced flavor. You can feel really full after eating just a small bowl of Phở trộn, maybe because of its genuine amount and quality that is passed into your stomach.

Serve: 5

Preparation Time: 30 minutes

Cooking Time: 30 minutes

Tricks: Make the dressing in advance.

FOR CHICKEN

- 600gr: Chicken Thigh
- 3-4 cloves: Shallot, smashed
- 1: Ginger, medium size, finely sliced
- 3-4 cloves: Garlic, smashed

- 1 Tbsp: Salt

FOR THE DRESSING
- 3 Tbsp: Tamarind juice
- 2 Tbsp: Fish Sauce
- 3 Tbsp: Coconut Sugar
- 3 Tbsp: Chicken Stock
- 1 tsp: Ginger, finely chopped
- 1 tsp: Garlic, finely chopped
- 1: Chili pepper, smashed

FOR THE ASSEMBLY
- 1 cup: Cucumber, thinly sliced
- 1 cup: Bean Sprout, boiled
- 2 Tbsp: Coriander, finely chopped
- 1 cup: Lettuce, thinly sliced
- ½ cup: Shallots+Garlic, thinly sliced, fried, drained
- ½ cup: Peanut, roasted, crushed
- 200 gr: Pho, boiled, drained well

In a saucepan, pour in 3 cups of water then add shallot, ginger, garlic and ¼ Tbsp salt. Bring to a boil. Let simmer for about 15-20 minutes over medium high heat.

Pour cold water in the saucepan, then add chicken and more cold water until the chicken is completely submerged. Add the rest of salt to the stock. Bring back to a boil over medium high heat. Reduce the heat to medium low and simmer for about 25 minutes (for small chicken about 1.2 kg) and 40-45 minutes for bigger one. Remember to flip over the chicken halfway through cooking until done. Remove from the heat and

transfer immediately to a big bowl of cold water. Let it sit for about 4-5 minutes. Remove from water.
Chop chicken into bite-sized pieces and set aside.
To make dressing: Combine almost all the ingredients, except chili pepper, and add to a small pot. Bring it to a simmer over medium heat for about 5 minutes until the sugar fully dissolves. Remove from the heat and set aside.
To assemble: Place about 1 cup of Pho in a serving bowl.
Drizzle chicken, herbs, pour dressing into the bowl.
Sprinkle fried shallots, garlic and roasted peanut on top.
Serve at room temperature or warm.
Mixed Pho Noodles – **Phở trộn**

'Thang' Noodle Soup

Bún Thang
Bún means Noodle, the meaning of Thang is still a question for many Vietnamese people because Thang, literally means Ladder, and doesn't really have any

connection with the food. There is a most reasonable explanation for this is that it has the influence from Chinese character where Thang is soup, Bún thang means "soup pours over noodles". Whatever meaning it carries, it is the most popular and favorite soup in Hanoi, the capital of Vietnam. The soup broth is very clear, fragrant, and tasty; the ingredients are diverse and colorful; the cooking process is subtle and sophisticated– from the preparation of ingredients preparation through cooking and assembling. In fact, there are many features that make up this dish, which is considered a most elegant, sophisticated food of Hanoi cuisine. When you look at the bowl of soup you may feel as if you are looking at a beautiful photograph. And believe me: once you have tried it, you will never forget it.

Serve: 4-5

Preparation Time: 30 minutes

Cooking Time: 1 hour

Tricks: use rock sugar for clear broth. Utilize the whole chicken with head and legs help to make the broth richer and sweeter. When boiling, uncover the lid so the broth becomes clearer. Chicken after boiling to be put right away in a bowl of cold water so the chicken's meat turns whiter and firmer.

FOR THE BROTH
- 3-4l: Water
- 2 tsp: Cooking Powder
- 1 pc: Onion, small size, cut into quarters
- 4 slices: Ginger

- 3 cloves: Garlic
- 1 tsp: Pepper Corn (optional)
- 1 ½ Tbsp: Dried Shrimp, toasted, rinsed well
- 2 heads: Dried Squid, toasted, rinsed well
- 2 tsp: Rock Sugar
- 1 ½ kg: Chicken, whole
- 5pcs: Shitake Dried Mushrooms (optional)

FOR ASSEMBLY
- 100gr: Vietnamese pork sausage **Giò lụa**
- 2: Eggs
- A handful: Knotgrass, chopped finely
- A handful: Spring Onions, chopped finely
- 2 Tbsp: Shrimp Paste
- 2 Tbsp: Lime
- 2 Tbsp: Sugar
- 1: Chili Pepper, finely chopped

SIDE-TABLE CONDIMENT

Shrimp paste mixed well with lime, sugar. Lime, Chili Sauce, Ground Pepper and Fish Sauce.

Rinse the chicken well. Then cut the head, legs and 2 small bones at the throat of the chicken. Toss together with onion, ginger, garlic, pepper and cooking powder into a deep saucepan. Pour in 3 cups of cold water. Bring to a boil. Then turn down the heat to low level and simmer for about half an hour.

After half an hour, add the rest of chicken into the saucepan. Add more cold water to the saucepan so that the water level covers the chicken, so it can be cooked evenly. Bring back to a boil on a medium high heat. Remove the foam layer. Then turn the heat to low level and cook gently for at 30 minutes until done, uncovered. Turn off the heat, Replace lid, and let the chicken sit for about 20 minutes, covered.

Add the beaten eggs with 1 tsp of fish sauce, a dash of sugar and black pepper. Stir well until there's no big chunks. Throw in just ½ tsp of Cooking Wine. Fry the omelette very thin in a skillet with a little oil. Let cool, fold the omelette then cut into very thin strips.

Remove the chicken from the broth. Add the drained dried shrimp, squid, rock sugar and shitake mushrooms and cook about 40 minutes on low heat. Let the chicken cool, then cut into thin strips or tear it into small pieces.

Adjust the taste of the broth by adding in 1 tsp fish sauce and/ or 1 tsp sugar.

To assemble: Put cooked noodles in a bowl, assemble with thin strips of chicken, sausage, eggs and garnish with herbs of Knotgrass, Spring Onions and Chopped Chili. Pour hot broth into the noodle bowl from the side of the bowl. Do not pour the broth directly into the center of the bowl.

Stir-Fry Glass Noodles With Crab Meat

Miến xào cua bể

Miến means Glass Noodles; Xào = Stir-fry; Cua (bể) is Crab

Miến xào cua bể has special significance to me, as it is one of the very first dishes that I learned to cook. The glass noodles are chewy but tender, the flavour is so aromatic and tasty, the sweetness and fragrance of the crab meat is unforgettable. Wow all those features combine together to make up a super umami, mouthwatering dish. I believe it will wake up all your senses when you try it.

Serve: 3-4

Preparation Time: 20 minutes

Cooking Time: 15 minutes

Tricks: Use glass noodles made of mung bean for a nice white color and tender, chewy outcome when cooked.

- 200g: Glass Noodles, soaked in warm water until soft, let it dry off

- 2Tbsp: Soy Sauce
- 200g: Crab Meat, fresh or canned
- 1: Carrot, peeled, julienned
- 100g: Celery, julienned
- 1: Onion, wedged
- 50g: Bean spouts
- a handful: Green Onion, cut into 2-3cm-length
- 3-4 cloves: Garlic, minced
- 1 Tbsp: Cooking Powder
- 1tsp: Sugar
- a dash: Ground Pepper
- Chicken Broth: to the need

Heat a wok with 3 Tbsps cooking oil and minced garlic over medium high heat until garlic turns golden brown. Remove the garlic with oil just leave a Tbsp on the wok. Add crab meat. Stir tenderly so it will not be beaten. Season with a dash of sugar, cooking powder and ground pepper. Sauté for about 1 more minute. Remove from the heat and transfer to a plate.

Mix the other 1 Tbsp of garlic oil (that we've made earlier) and soy sauce with glass noodles. Set it aside.

Bring the wok back to a heat. Add the rest of the garlic oil to the wok. Add carrot, onion, celery and bean sprouts. Stir to mix. Season with 1Tbsp of cooking powder. Mix well. You can always add more chicken broth if the mixture gets dry.

Make some room in the centre of the wok and add glass noodles. Toss constantly for about 4-5 minutes and cook over medium high heat until the glass noodles are coated evenly with seasoning and turn translucent. Add half the crab meat and chopped green onion. Toss again. Remove from heat.

To assemble: Transfer glass noodles with vegetables and crab to a serving plate. Drizzle with the last half of crab meat and sprinkle with ground pepper on top. Serve at room temperature or warm.

Hue-Style Beef Vermicelli Noodles Soup

Bún bò Huế

Vermicelli Noodles = Bún; Beef is Bò; Hue-style means this soup originally comes from Hue, in central Vietnam.

Bún bò Huế is considered the second-best soup of Vietnamese cuisine. This dish is a great example of how the right balance of spicy, sour, salty and sweet flavors together with lemongrass can be surprisingly delicious. Additionally, tons of fresh herbs with tender slices of beef on top are really the cherries on this dish. It takes some time and a little effort to cook, but it will worth it!

Serve: 5
Preparation Time: 30 minutes
Cooking Time: 2 hours
Tricks: The herbs should be dipped in the stock for only 15-20 minutes so their flavour can be fully kept in the broth.

- 500g: Beef Bones, rinsed well, chopped into 5cm-length
- 500g: Beef, tender loin or shank
- 500g: Pork Knuckles (optional), chopped into bite-sized pieces, dipped into boiling water for about 30 seconds, then wash clean. Set aside.
- 8 cups: Water
- 3: Lemongrass, smashed
- ¼: Pineapple, finely sliced
- ½ Tbsp: Salt
- 1Tbsp: Cooking Seasoning
- 2Tbsp: Sugar, rock
- ½ Tbsp: Fish Sauce
- 1Tbsp: Chili Oil
- 2Tbsp: Annatto Oil (optional)
- 1 ½ Tbsp: Salted Shrimp Paste

To serve with
- 1: Lime
- 1: Chili Pepper
- 1: Onion, thinly sliced
- a handful: Coriander, finely cut
- a handful: Green Onion, finely cut
- a handful: Sawtooth (optional), finely cut

Mixture of fresh vegetables of your choice including: banana flower shredded, Thai basil, bean sprout, Vietnamese coriander, onion etc.

In a big saucepan, pour 8 cups water in and add beef bones, beef shank and pork knuckles. Bring to a boil over high heat. Then reduce the heat to medium low and simmer for about 1 ½ hours until the shank gets tender and the flavour is released from bones. Remove bones, shank and knuckles from the broth. Place shank and knuckles in a cold water for about 1 minute then let dry. Cut shank into think slices. Set it aside.

Add lemongrass and pineapple to the broth. Let it cook for about 15 minutes over medium high heat.

In a small pot, pour a cup of water in, add shrimp paste and stir to mix. Let cook for about 30 minutes over medium heat in order to reduce the sickly smell. Turn off the heat and pour the clear water over the shrimp paste pot into the broth.

Season the broth with salt, cooking seasoning, fish sauce, sugar and chili oil. Bring back to a boil. Then remove from heat.

To assemble: Place noodles in a serving bowl. Add 3-4 slices of beef shank, 1-2 pork knuckles; Garnish with onion slices. Top with chopped coriander, green onion and sawtooth. Sprinkle with ground pepper on top.

Ladle the hot broth over the face until it is almost full. Add vegetables and squeeze the lime juice to your taste. Serve at room temperature or warm.

Vermicelli Noodles With Tilapia

Bún cá rô

Vermicelli Noodles mean Bún; Tilapia is Cá rô.

Bún cá rô is a common breakfast-noodles soup cooked with common and simple ingredients like tilapia or mackerel, water parsley, dill, green onion. But it tastes super delicious. The soup is clear and sweet; The fish dough are chewy, elastic and full of dill-and-fish flavour.

Serve: 4-5

Preparation Time: 1h30 minutes

Cooking Time: 30 minutes

Tricks: in order to make the fish dough elastic, freeze the fish before blending. Using the technique of single click-release at a time also helps the elasticity.

FOR THE DOUGH
- 400g: Tilapia (or Mackerel), fillet, cut into 1.5cm cubes, frozen
- 1Tbsp: Fish Sauce

- 1tsp: Seasoning
- 1 ½ tsp: Sugar
- ½ tsp: Ground Pepper
- 2 cloves: Garlic, peeled
- 1Tbsp: Green Onion including white part, finely cut
- ½ cup: Dill, finely cut
- 1Tbsp: Cooking Oil
- 1Tbsp: Corn Flour
- 1tsp: Baking Powder

FOR THE REST
- 1: Ginger, medium size, smashed
- 1Tbsp: Fish Sauce
- ½ tsp: Salt
- 1tsp: Sugar
- 2 cups: Water Parsley, cut into 3finger-length pieces, dip into a boiling water for about 30 seconds. Remove from the heat, set it aside for serving with noodles.
- 400g: Noodles, boiled, soaked for 8-10minutes, rinse under running water, let it dry
- 1 cup: Shallots, finely sliced, deep fried over low heat until golden

In a blender, combine all the ingredients for making fish dough except corn flour and baking powder. When you blend, remember not to warm the fish. Don't let the motor run continuously until the mixture is finely ground. Instead, single click and release at a time… After about 5 minutes, transfer the mixture into a bowl. Add corn flour and baking powder, mix well slowly for about 10 minutes. Then transfer back to the blender. Repeat the click-release process for about 5 minutes. Remove from the blender and mix by your hand again for about 10 more minutes and with quicker speed than the first time until all the ingredients are fully integrated with each other.

Divide the mixture into different dough, shape of your choice. Use cling film wrap each dough and shape into a flat cake. Put in the freezer for about half hour.

Heat a frying pan with 3 cups of cooking oil over medium high heat. You can test the heat by dipping your chopsticks in the pan. When the bubbles appear around the chopsticks, place fish dough in. Flip frequently until 2 sides of the dough turn golden brown. Then remove fish dough from the heat. Let it cool completely, then cut into 2cm-width strips.

Pour 2l of water into a saucepan, add fish bone and head. Let it simmer for about 40-45 minutes until the sweetness is released. Use the strainer to strain the solid pieces to make the broth clear. Bring it back to a boil. Add ginger, and let it cook for about 10 minutes. Turn of the heat then add spices. First add sugar, followed with salt, then add fish sauce last.

Place 100g of noodles in a large bowl, put fish strips, water, and parsley in separate corners. Pour the broth onto the bowl. Sprinkle green onion, dill, ground pepper and fried shallot on top. Serve warm or at room temperature.

Bún cá rô – **Tilapia Noodles**

Vermicelli Noodles With Stir-Fry Beef

Bún thịt bò xào

Vermicelli Noodles mean Bún; Stir fry is Xào; Beef is Bò or thịt Bò.

Vietnamese Vermicelli Noodles with stir fry beef is worth a try in summer time. Refreshing noodles are served with a lot of fresh herbs and juicy beef, then topped with pickled vegetables, chopped peanuts, and drenched in fish sauce really bring you a delicious, healthy and easy-to-eat meal.

Serve: 4-5

Preparation Time: 15 minutes

Cooking Time: 1 hour

Tricks: Coat beef evenly with corn flour so that the beef holds onto all of the sweetness and flavor, and stays tender and juicy. Prepare all of your ingredients and dipping sauce before you start to stir fry to save time and serve fresh right after cooking.

FOR MARINATING THE BEEF

- 400g: Beef fillet or skirt, thinly sliced
- 2 cloves: Garlic, minced
- 1 tsp: Shallot, minced
- 1 tsp: Soy Sauce
- 1 tsp: Oyster Sauce
- 1 tsp: Chicken Powder
- 1 tsp: Sugar
- ½ tsp: Ground Pepper
- 2 Tbsp: Lemongrass, finely chopped lemongrass (white part only)
- 1-2Tbsp: Corn Flour
- 1 Tbsp: Veg.oil

FOR NOODLE SALAD
- 454g: Packet of vermicelli noodles, cook as per instructions on packet
- 1 cup: Bean sprouts
- 1: Cucumber, halved and sliced into batons
- 2 cups: Vietnamese herbs (perilla leaves, mint leaves and Vietnamese mint leaves), finely chopped
- 2 Tbsp: Vegetable oil
- 1: Small Onion, cut into strips
- 1 cup: Pickled carrot and white radish (optional)
- 1/4 cup: Peanuts, roasted, crushed

FOR DIPPING SAUCE
- 2 Tbsp: Fish Sauce
- 2 Tbsp: Sugar or Honey
- 2-3 Tbsp: Lime Juice
- 8 Tbsp: Water
- 3 cloves: Garlic, minced

- 1: Chili Pepper, finely chopped

Make the dipping sauce: Combine all the ingredients for making dipping sauce in a bowl, and stir well until fully dissolved.

Cook the vermicelli noodles, wash and slice the herbs and cucumber. Divide your vermicelli noodles into bowls followed by herbs, sprouts and cucumber and set aside.

Combine the ingredients for marinating beef in a small bowl. Add the mixture to the beef and marinate for about 15 minutes.

To sauté: Heat the wok. Add the oil and chopped garlic. Stir well until garlic is golden brown. Finally, add the beef to the wok. Toss until it turns brown, let sauté for about 1-2minutes over high heat until done.

To assemble: Drizzle the beef on top of the ready-prepared noodle bowls.

Dress with pickled vegetables, crushed peanuts, fried onions and serve with dipping sauce.

Spring Roll

Nem rán/Chả giò

Vietnamese Spring Rolls are an example of the most classic Vietnamese cuisine, very popular around the world nowadays. Many countries also have their own versions of spring rolls in their cuisine, but the Vietnamese spring roll stands out because it includes different ingredients including special rice paper to wrap the spring roll. This recipe is based on the palate of Northern Vietnamese which is the most preferential and influential version of spring rolls in Vietnam.

Serve: 3-4

Preparation Time: 30-45 minutes

Cooking time: Fry 30 minutes the first time. Fry a second time for more crispy result.

Special tool: frying-pan or wok, chopsticks for frying

Tricks: Use hand towel to soften the rice paper. Put some drops of lemon juice onto the oil pan before frying. Fold the rolls tightly.

FOR THE FILLING
- 1kg: Minced Pork Shoulder, finely chopped by hand
- 5-6 gloves: Shallots, small siz2, thinly julienned
- 3: Fungus, medium size, soaked then julienned
- 5-6: Dried Shiitake, small size, soaked then julienned
- 1 cup: Jicama
- 2: Onions
- 1: Carrot, big, julienned
- 1: Eggs, small size
- 100g: Glass Noodles
- 1tsp: Seasoning Powder

- 1tsp: Fish Sauce
- 1 ½ Tbsp: Spring Onions, chopped
- ½ tsp: Ground Pepper
- 300gr: Shrimp, (optional), chopped
- As needed: Cooking oil

FOR THE DIPPING SAUCE
- 3-4 gloves: Garlic
- 1: Chilli pepper
- 2 Tbsp: Sugar
- 2 ½ Tbsp: Fish Sauce
- 1 ½ Tbsp: Lime juice
- 1 ½ Tbsp: Vinegar
- 5Tbsp: Water
- 1/4 tsp: Ground Pepper
- ½ cup: Carrot, thinly sliced, soaked in salt for about 10 minutes. Rinsed well by boiling water. Drain well.
- ½ cup: Finely sliced Kohlrabi, thinly sliced, soaked in salt for about 10 minutes. Rinsed well by boiling water. Drain well.

To make the Filling: Combine all the ingredients for making the filling in a large bowl and mix until well blended. Set aside.

To wrap the rolls: Dip two hand towels in a bowl of warm water then squeeze out as much water as possible. Put rice paper onto one of the towels then cover it with the second towel. Let it sit for about 3-4 seconds until the rice paper softens. Remove and place on a dry surface, then smooth it with your fingers. Add about 1Tbsp of the Filling onto the rice paper. Fold one end of the wrapper over the Filling, then fold the sides and roll up tightly, pressing to seal. Repeat until all the ingredients are used.

To make dipping sauce: Pound the garlic then transfer to a bowl. Add chopped chili pepper. Add the water, sugar, fish sauce, and lime juice and mix well until the sugar dissolves. Finally, add daikon and carrot. Sprinkle with ground black pepper.

To fry the rolls: Fill the oil up to 1.5 finger breadths into a non-stick frying pan then heat it over medium heat. Add a few drops of lemon juice into the pan. Put the spring rolls, a few at a time, in the hot pan for about 5 minutes until golden brown then flip to brown each side. Don't flip continuously just flip when one side almost done. When done, slide it onto paper towel to absorb excess oil. Cut the spring rolls into bite sizes.

Place the spring rolls on a serving platter and serve with noodles and a mix of fragrant leaves, lettuce, bean sprouts, Carrot and Radish Pickles and a bowl of Fish Sauce Dip on the side.

Nem Hà Nội – **Ha Noi's version Spring Roll**

Note:
There are regional variations to this recipe. For example: In Haiphong, a city one-hour north of Hanoi, they make spring rolls by adding more crab meat into the filling and shaping the roll into a square. Meanwhile, people in the south of Vietnam prefer to change the components of the filling by replacing bean

root with taro and keeping the size of the roll smaller. The smaller size together with the cooked taro, helps to absorb the excess liquid inside the filling make the rolls come out crispier and with more umami.

Nem Hải Phòng – **Hai Phong's version Spring Roll**

Summer Rolls

Gỏi cuốn

Gỏi cuốn is a traditional Southern Vietnamese dish which is full of fresh and healthy ingredients with the amount of veggies balanced with protein from the shrimp and pork.

You can find many versions of rolls in different countries around the world. From China, with a wrapper made of wheat and duck, filled with cucumber and ginger to Thailand, which makes a summer roll using similar protein ingredients to the Vietnamese version, but with a different dipping sauce and vegetables.

Gỏi cuốn, the Vietnamese summer roll, uses rice paper as a wrapper for the roll. The filling consists of pork meat, prawn, vegetables, and rice vermicelli. The distinction that makes the Vietnamese roll stand out from the crowd lies in the variety of dipping sauces served with this dish. There are three primary dipping sauces: hoisin-peanut based sauce, Anchovy sauce and sweet sour sauce. Summer rolls are considered to be a very popular appetizer with customers in Vietnamese restaurants.

Serve: 3-4
Preparation Time: 45 minutes
Cooking Time: 45 min (including 15 preparation time)
Trick: Wrap the roll tightly.

FOR THE FILLING
- 300 gr: Pork Belly/Pork leg
- 1 tsp: Cooking powder
- 2 gloves: shalotts
- 200 gr: Shrimps 15 pcs
- 200 gr: Rice vermicelli "bún"
- 15 pcs: Rice paper (22 cm/ 8.7 in diameter)
- A handful: Fresh greens of your choice but lettuce, mint, cilantro are needed. Basil is not recommended for this dish.

FOR THE DIPPING SAUCE
- 1 tsp: Cooking Oil
- 1 tsp: Garlic, minced
- 3 Tbsp: Hoisin sauce
- 5 Tbsp: Broth from boiling Pork and Prawn
- 1.5 Tbsp: Peanut Butter

- 1 Tbsp: Tamarind juice
- 1 tsp: Honey
- 1 tsp: Chili Pepper, minced
- 1 tsp: Roasted Peanuts, crushed

Rinse the pork meat thoroughly. Bring it to a boil in a large pot with cooking powder and shallots. Cook on medium high heat until fully cooked. Remove from broth.

De-vein the prawn then wash again until clean. Throw prawn in pork broth and bring to a boil for 1-2 minutes on medium-high heat. Let cool and peel. Slice each shrimp lengthwise into 2 halves. Rinse again if there are still black lines until cleared.

Put rice vermicelli in a big bowl. Pour boiling water into the bowl. Let it sit for 8 to 10 minutes until soft. Rinse the noodles under cold water to remove the starch. Drain dry.

To make dipping sauce: Heat cooking oil in a small saucepan on medium high heat, then fry the minced garlic until golden brown. Add hoisin sauce, pork & prawn broth and peanut butter. Stir well, then add tamarind sauce and honey. Stir again and simmer on low heat for 1-2 minutes, uncovered, until slightly thickened. Pour the sauce into condiment bowls and top with minced fresh chili and crushed peanuts.

To assemble the roll: Place the cooked rice vermicelli, shrimps, meat, fresh greens and sliced cucumber on the plates.

For rice paper wrapper: Use the same technique used to make spring rolls by using 2 hand towels, or dip rice paper in a pan of lukewarm water to soften. If using this technique, dip one piece of rice paper into the water, covering the paper with water without soaking it. Then, gently shake off the excess water.

Prepare a flat work surface like a cutting board or a large plate, for rolling. After softening the rice paper, lay it on the flat surface. Organize the roll by into layers. Place the fresh vegetables on the first layer in a row on the lower or upper third of the rice paper, leaving about 2 fingers on both sides. Next, place 2-3 slices of vermicelli and 2 prawn halves in front of the layers of vegetables and noodles so prawn and meat can be seen from the outside of the end product. Keep the orange side of prawn facing down.

Fold 2 sides of the roll first then the end closest to the fillings, roll over the noodles then keep rolling tightly until you reach the center of the rice paper. Add some garlic chives on to give the roll a little "tail. Continue rolling until done.

Serve with different side-table dipping sauces: hoisin-peanut based, anchovy sauce, or sweet & sour, depending on your palate.

How to wrap a roll

Beef Wrapped In Betel Leaves

Bò cuốn lá lốt
Bò = Beef; Cuốn is wrap; Lá lốt = Betel Leaves.
Betel Leaves growing throughout Vietnam, and are used for foods and medicine. The leaves are very fragrant and even more fragrant when they are heated. Beef wrapped in Betel Leaves is the most favorite "wrap & roll" food in the south of Vietnam. This dish has a perfect balance of texture and taste, meat and veggies, as well as a number of great ways of enjoying and wrapping, and a harmonious combination of all 5 fundamental elements of Viet cuisine. With its amazing features, including flavors of saltiness, spiciness and bitterness, Bò cuốn lá lốt works very well with beer or wine.
Yields: 3-4
Cooking Time: 30 minutes
Preparation Time: 30 minutes
Tricks: The rolls should be small so you can only grill or half-fry betel leaves for about just 5 minutes each side

until the leaves stick together with the fillings and the color of the leaves is still green. Do not let them overcook or turn dark brown, because overcooking causes betel leaves to become bitter.

FOR BEEF MARINATING
- 250g: Beef, any kinds, minced
- 100g: Pork, much fat, minced
- 1Tbsp: Soy Sauce
- 1 ½ tsp: Seasoning
- 2tsp: Sugar
- ½ tsp: Ground Pepper
- 3 cloves: Garlic, minced
- 2tsp: Lemongrass, minced

FOR WRAPPING
- 25-30: Betel Leaves, big size, even

Vegetable Oil is enough for half-fry.

You can also grill up the dish by using char grill or barbecue hotplate over medium heat. In this case you should rub a bit of oil on the betel roll to keep it moist and cook for about 5 minutes each side.

FOR DIPPING SAUCE
- 2Tbsp: Anchovy Sauce, commercial
- ½ cup: Pineapple, finely chopped
- 2Tbsp: Sugar, granulated
- 5Tbsp: Warm Water
- 1tsp: Garlic, minced
- 1tsp: Chili Pepper, minced

FOR THE REST
- 2Tbsp: Peanuts, roasted, crushed
- 1/3 cup: Melted lard: **see note**

- 200g: Fine Rice Vermicelli

Mix of Vegetables: Lettuce, Coriander, Mint, Perilla, Cucumber etc.

Note: How to make Melted Lard:

Prepare a bowl of 1Tbsp of spring onion, finely chopped and a dash of salt, sugar, seasoning.

Heat 2Tbsp of oil in a pot. Pour into the bowl. Add more cool vegetable oil of about 1Tbsp. Stir well.

Combine all the ingredients for marinating beef in a bowl and mix well. Let it sit for about 15-20 minutes.

Wash clean betel leaves. Lay the leaves flat on a cloth to dry. Cut the stem of the leaves to ½ cm short.

To wrap the rolls, lay two betel leaves, shiny side down, on a board with the stem of a leaf pointing towards you. Spoon approximately 1 tsp of the beef mixture onto the bottom half of the leaf. Fold slowly, tightly up over the meat and use the stem to seal it up. Repeat this process until all the beef is used.

To make dipping sauce: Add pineapple in a bowl, add anchovy sauce, sugar. Mix well. Leave it aside. When you are ready to be served, add warm water, minced garlic and chili pepper.

There are numerous ways of cooking:

Half-fry: Heat an amount of oil for half-fry in a frying pan (flat pan). Add beef rolls, a few at a time. Let cook for about 5 minutes each side over medium heat, uncovered. Remove from the heat.

Grill: Heat a charcoal grill. Grill the rolls for about 5 minutes each side, uncovered.

Broil: Preheat to broil. Place the beef rolls on the baking sheet and slip into the oven and broil for approximately 5-6 minutes depending on the oven. Check and turn them frequently to ensure they are cooking evenly and avoid the burning of the leaves.

To assemble: Transfer beef rolls onto a serving platter. Top with melted lard and crushed roasted peanuts. Serve with a mix of vegetables, wrap with fine vermicelli and dip in fermented anchovy sauce.

Bò cuốn lá lốt – **Beef wrapped in Betel Leaves**

Rice Dishes

In Vietnam, most dishes are designed to be served with rice or rice related-dishes. Unlike westerners who eat bread day after day, rice is the main carbohydrate for our meals.

Rice is an object of worship in Viet culture. Yes, rice is a big thing out here. In ancient Vietnam, rice is the image of many rice plants and a square symbolizing a paddy field. Accordingly, many main dishes and snacks in Vietnam are made from rice: boiled rice in daily meal, rice porridge, steamed rice, glutinous rice cake. And traditional cake Banh Chung (square cake) which is made of glutinous rice and wrapped in a green square package, symbolizes the Earth. Similar to it, another variation of glutinous rice dish named Banh Day which is made into a round shape, symbolizes the God. Rice is extremely important to Vietnamese people and customs.

A Street Rice Stall In Hochiminh City

Honey Lime Fried Chicken

Gà rán tẩm mật ong và chanh
Gà = Chicken; Rán means Fry; Mật ong is Honey; Chanh: Lime
Actually, this is not a typical Vietnamese dish, but I make it due to the influence of the sour and sweet tastes coming from honey and lime, which you can often taste in chicken or fowl or game dishes in Vietnamese cuisine.
Serve: 5
Preparation Time: 5 minutes
Cooking Time: 20 minutes

Tricks: You can use lime peel instead of lime leaf for a similar result.

FOR THE SAUCE
- 2Tbsp: Honey
- 1: Chili Pepper
- ¼ tsp: Ground Pepper, white
- ½ Tbsp: Fish Sauce
- a touch: Salt
- 1: Lime Leaves, thinly sliced
- 2Tbsp: Freshly squeezed lime juice
- 1tsp: Annatto oil

FOR THE REST
- 750g: Chicken Thigh
- Cucumber: To the need
- Tomato: To the need

To make the sauce: Combine all the ingredients for making sauce into a bowl, mix well. Leave it aside.

Heat a frying pan over medium high heat, place chicken thigh in and fry for about 3-5 minutes on each side until it turns golden brown and crispy. Remove the extra oil in the pan.

Pour the sauce mixture into the pan, mix well until the chicken is coated evenly with sauce. Let simmer for about 5-10 minutes over low heat until well cooked. Remove from the heat.

To assemble, place cucumber and tomato slices on the side of a serving plate. Transfer chicken to this plate. Serve at room temperature or warm.

Honey Lime Fried Chicken - **Gà rán tẩm mật ong và chanh**

Caramelized Pork & Egg

Thịt kho trứng
Thịt = Pork, Meat; Kho = Caramelized; Egg = Trứng
Yields: 4-5
Preparation Time: 1 hour
Cooking time: 2 ½ to 3 hours
Special Tool: a big sauce pan, chopsticks
Tricks:
-      Make the dish a day in advance and reheat at the time of serving to let eggs and pork absorb the flavor and get nice brown color.
-      Do not use 100% of coconut water for cooking as the glaze will turn sour when cooked.
- 5-6 gloves: Shallots
- 3-4 gloves: Garlic
- 4-5: Green Onion, white part
- 1-2: Chili Peppers

- 2/3 tsp: Salt
- 1 Tbsp: Brown Sugar
- 1 Tbsp: Fish Sauce
- 2-3 cup: Coconut water
- 4-6 cups: Water
- ½ kg: Pork Belly
- ½ kg: Pork Leg
- 6 pcs: Eggs, hard-boiled
- 1 Tbsp: Cilantro, green onions for garnish

To marinate the pork, slice pork belly and pork leg into 1-inch pieces, and transfer to a bowl.

Chop shallots, white part of green onion and garlic finely; Smash chili pepper then add all the herbs to the pork's bowl. Add salt, then massage the pork well with herbs and salt so it can be evenly covered. Let it rest for about an hour in the fridge.

To caramelize pork and eggs:

After one hour, take the pork out of the fridge. Pour coconut water into a big pot. Add the marinated pork. Add about 4-6 cups of water to the pot to ensure the water and coconut cover the pork so the pork can be cooked evenly. Bring it to a boil. Skim the dirt from the surface of the broth. Finally, turn down the heat to low, and simmer for about 2 hours, covered.

Boil the Eggs: In a small pot, add 1 ½ cup of cool water and eggs in. Stir the eggs in circle in order to keep the yolk in the middle. Bring it to a boil over medium high heat. Turn down the heat to medium-low, and keep eggs boiling for 10 minutes. Take out and cool immediately in a bowl of cold water. Peel the eggs.

After 2 hours of simmering, add the eggs to the pork pot, and bring to a boil. Season with 1Tbsp Fish Sauce and 1Tbsp Brown Sugar. Toss well. Simmer, covered, for another 1 hour until pork and eggs turn tender, coated evenly and turn a golden brown color. Remove from the heat. Top with chopped coriander and green onion. Serve with cooked rice.

Caramelized Fish In Clay Pot

Cá kho tộ

Cá = Fish; Kho is Caramelized; Tộ is called by the southern Vietnamese like a Clay Pot.

Cá kho tộ is a common daily dish of people in the south of Vietnam. The flavor is tasty, and the fish is super soft when cooked. This dish is perfectly suitable for serving with steamed rice.

Serve: 3-4

Preparation Time: 1-2 hours

Cooking Time: 30 minutes

Tricks: Make the dish the day before serving to let the fish absorb the flavor.

FOR FISH MARINATING
- 300gr: Basa Fish or Seabass, cut into 3-4cm length pieces
- a dash: Salt
- a dash: Seasoning
- ¼ tsp: Sugar

- ¼ tsp: Black Pepper
- ½ tsp: Fish Sauce
- ¼ tsp: MSG
- 1 ½ tsp: Chili Flakes

FOR PORK MARINATING
- 100gr: Pork Belly, slice thinly
- ½ tsp: Fish Sauce
- ½ tsp: Seasoning Powder
- ¼ tsp: Ground Pepper

FOR THE REST
- 2Tbsp: Fish Sauce
- 1 ½ Tbsp: Brown Sugar
- 1 tsp: Dark or Black Soy Sauce
- 1 Tbsp: Spring Onions, green part, chopped finely
- 1 Tbsp: Spring Onions, white part, julienned
- 3 cloves: Garlic, minced

To marinate fish: In a big bowl, combine all the ingredients. Let it sit for about 1-2 hours.

To marinate pork: In a small bowl, combine all the ingredient. Let it sit for about 1-2 hour.

To caramelize: Heat a clay pot. Or if you don't have a clay pot, you can use a medium pot, with 1Tbsp of cooking oil and 1Tbsp sugar over medium high heat until the sugar browns. Pour 1 Tbsp fish sauce in, then add pork. Stir to mix and let cook for about 1-2 minutes until the fat begins to separate. Make a hole in the middle and place fish in. Add 1Tbsp fish sauce, 2/3 Tbsp sugar and a cup of water. Bring the pot back to a boil over medium high heat. Then reduce the heat to medium low and cook for about 30 minutes, covered.

Place smashed chili peppers and green-part onion, drizzle with ground pepper on top. Remove from the heat.
Serve with cooked rice.

Steamed Fish With Dill

Cá Hấp Thì Là
Cá = fish; Hấp means steamed; Thì là is dill.
In this dish, the whole fish is steamed with sweet, sour and dill sauce with dill as the major flavor. The taste is quite balanced, delicious, and refreshing. In addition, it takes just a short time to cook so it's really a good choice for daily meals for you and your family.
Serve: 3-4
Time: 15-20 minutes
Special Tool: a Steamer
Tricks: Make the dressing a day before serving and keep in the fridge.
FOR DRESSING
- 1Tbsp: Honey
- 1 ½ Tbsp: Fish Sauce
- 2Tbsp: Lime Juice
- 2Tbsp: Water
- 1: Chili Pepper, finely chopped
- 2 cloves: Garlic, minced

- 1Tbsp: Dill, finely chopped

FOR THE REST

- 800g: Sea bass, whole, cleaned, sprinkle with a touch of salt and ground pepper
- 5-6: Dill, whole (with roots)
- 4-5 slices: Ginger

In a bowl, combine the ingredients for making dressing except dill and garlic, and mix well until honey fully dissolves. Top with minced garlic and chopped dill. Leave the dressing aside.

Put 5-6 dill roots into the tummy of the fish; Dill leaves and ginger slices on the body of the sea bass. Use a steamer to steam for about 10 minutes. Remove from the heat and transfer sea bass to a serving plate. Pour dressing over it. Serve in room temperature or warm.

Braised Chicken With Shiitake Mushroom

Thịt gà kho nấm

Braised: Kho; Chicken means Gà; Mushroom is Nấm. Braised Chicken with Shiitake Mushroom is a tasty dish, which comes from the aroma of herbs like mushroom and ginger. Like many other foods containing ginger, this dish is most suitable for the winter season, when it helps to keep you warm on cold days.

Serve: 3-4

Preparation Time: 1 hour

Cooking Time: 45 minutes

Tricks: Use chicken thigh to make this dish more chewy, and hence, more delicious.

FOR DRESSING
- 1 Tbsp: Soy Sauce
- 2/3 Tbsp: Cooking Powder
- 1 tsp: Sugar, granulated
- 1-2 Tbsp: Water
- 2 Tbsp: Oyster Sauce
- 1 Tbsp: Ginger, cut into thin strips

FOR THE REST
- 500g: Chicken Thigh, rinsed, cut in to bite-sized pcs
- 3 cloves: Garlic, minced
- 1-2: Chili Pepper, smashed
- 2/3 cup: Shiitake Mushroom, soaked, washed clean, finely sliced
- 1: Carrot, medium size, peeled, finely sliced
- 1: Onion, small size, peeled, cut into wedges
- 2 Tbsp: Vegetable Oil
- 2 Tbsp: Coriander, Green Onion, finely chopped
- ½ tsp: Ground Pepper

In a wok or a skillet, add Vegetable oil. Throw in garlic, stirring constantly for about 1-2 minutes until golden brown. Add in shitake mushroom and toss well. Add chicken. Season with mix of dressing. Let simmer for about 15 minutes on medium low heat.

Add carrot then onions, and stir well. Add ginger. Let cook for about another 5 minutes, then turn off the heat and transfer to a serving bowl.

To assemble, transfer stir-fried chicken with vegetables to a plate. Drizzle with chopped coriander and green onions. Sprinkle ground pepper on top. Serve with cooked rice and hot soup.

Salty And Spicy Grilled Chicken Wings

Cánh gà nướng muối ớt

Cánh gà = chicken wings; Nướng means grill; Muối is salt and Ớt = chili pepper

Cánh gà nướng muối ớt particularly works well with alcohol because the only flavors in this dish are saltiness and spiciness, which contrast with the acidity and sweetness of alcohol. It is also a very simple dish; It doesn't require much time at all, so it's perfectly suitable for you on busy days.

Serve: 4-5

Preparation Time: 10 minutes

Cooking Time: 10 minutes

Tricks: You should marinate the chicken one day in advance for the best result.

- 10: Chicken wings, cut into 2 parts lengthwise
- ½ Tbsp: Salt
- ½ Tbsp: Seasoning
- 1Tbsp: Brown Sugar

- 1 tsp: Ground Pepper
- 1Tbsp: Garlic Powder
- 2: Chili Pepper, pounded

Combine all the ingredients in a large bowl. Massage chicken wings well to coat with spices, particularly chili pepper. Let it sit for at least 3 hours, or better, overnight in the fridge.

Heat an oven at 190oC, 10 minutes before putting the chicken wings in. roast for 20 minutes then bring them out and flip to the other side. Bring back to the oven and roast for another 20 minutes or until chicken wings turn golden brown. Remove from the oven.

Serve with cooked rice or alone.

Mocked Dog Meat

Giả cầy

Giả = mocked; Cầy or Chó means Dog

This dish is a specialty in Hanoi, but it is also popular in other parts of Vietnam. Viet people often serve it in winter time or chilly days. According to oriental medicine, pork meat has the coolness, which is one of the 5 fundamental senses in cuisine, while galangal and pepper add the heat. The harmonious combination of the contrasting elements in this dish reflects the yin-yang relationship and thus it's good for health. The bold flavor of galangal and shrimp paste, together with the refreshing sourness of fermented rice and the fragrance of savory pork make it one of the most popular dishes in Vietnam.

Yields: 3-4

Preparation time: 30 minutes

Cooking time: 30-45 minutes

Tricks: Pig trotters should be partially grilled the outside before cooking so it they will be more fragrant. They should not be cut into small pieces as they will shrink a lot after cooking.

FOR MARINATING

- 1: Pig Trotters, calf, cut into bite-sized pieces
- 1(roughly 1/2cup): Galangal, soaked for about 1 hour, minced
- a dash: Salt, Sugar, Ground Pepper, MSG, Fish Sauce
- 1Tbsp: Shrimp Paste
- 3Tbsp: Fermented Cold Rice
- 1Tbsp: Vegetable Oil

FOR THE REST
- 1½ Tbsp: Vegetable Oil
- 3-4 cups: Water, cover the pork
- 1 cup: Fresh Bamboo Shoots
- a handful: Buffalo Spinach, Sawtooth Coriander, finely chopped
- 1 cup: Banana Flower (Optional), discard the outside old, firm leaves; julienned; soak in lightly salty water for about 15-20 minutes to reduce the bitterness and the darkness; dried.

To marinate pig, combine all the ingredients for marinating into a big bowl, mix well and let it rest in the fridge overnight. Or if you would like to cook right after marinating, just let the mixture sit for about 5-10 minutes without vegetable oil.

To cook, heat oil in a pot and add the mixture. Toss well and let cook for about 8-9 minutes over medium high heat until the pork absorbs the spices. Pour water in the pot, add bamboo shoot, and bring the pot back to a boil. Reduce the heat to medium low heat and simmer for at least half an hour or until the pork turns tender. Adjust to your taste. Remove from the heat. Transfer the dish to a serving plate, sprinkle with buffalo spinach and sawtooth coriander on top. Serve with rice noodles or cooked rice.

Note: If you use banana leaves instead of bamboo shoot, you add it just 4-5 minutes before done.

Jellied Pork
Thịt nấu đông

Thịt (lợn) = Pork; Nấu đông is Jellied.

The texture of Jellied Pork is created naturally if you let it sit in room temperature in cold weather, so it's particularly convenient if you make this dish in winter. The meat when cooked is super tender and delicious; the taste is milder than braised pork but stronger than boiled. The star of the dish is fish sauce which really brings out the fragrance for the dish.

Serve: 4-5
Preparation Time: 20-30 minutes
Cooking Time: 1 hour
Tricks: In order to clear the pork meat away from dirt and smell, clean it with a mixture of water, salt, and white wine. Adding more pork skin (the ratio to the meat is about ¼ or 2/3) helps the dish concentrate or become 'jelly' more easily and the texture is firmer.
FOR MARINATING PORK
- 400g: Pork Leg meat with skin, cut into thin small slices
- 100g: Pork Skin
- 2Tbsp: Fish Sauce
- a pinch: Salt
- a pinch: Sugar
- a pinch: MSG
- ½ tsp: Ground Pepper

FOR THE REST
- 2 cups: Water
- 1-2: Fungus, soaked, cleaned, julienned

To marinate the pork, combine all the ingredients for marinating pork in a big bowl. Mix well. Allow it marinade for about 1-2 hours in the fridge.

Transfer the pork to a big saucepan. Pour water in and bring it to a boil on high heat. Remove sponges to clear the broth. Add fungus, stir well. Bring back to a boil. Then turn down the heat to medium low heat and simmer for at least ½ hour until the meat turns tender. Season to taste, and remove from heat.

To assemble, transfer the dish to a bowl to ensure that the broth covers the meat and fungus completely. Let it cool to room temperature, then put in the fridge until it concentrates like a jelly. When you serve, take the jellied pork out of the fridge, turn the bowl upside down, and use a knife the remove it from the bowl. You can cut into your favorite shaped chunks but they should be big. Otherwise, they may break, as the texture is not very firm. Just leave enough for each serving at room temperature. The residual should be stored back in the fridge to keep its shape.

Shrimp Roasted With Salt

Tôm rang muối
Tôm = Shrimp; Rang = Roast; Muối is Salt.
Shrimp roasted with salt is a super yummy dish, perfect for serving with cooked rice or eaten alone. It takes very short time and it is very easy to make, so it's also suitable for a quick meal.
Serve: 3-4
Time: 10-15 minutes
Tips: - A good way to make the food less fatty, is to add a mix of vegetables, thus improving the balance of the dish.
Shrimp doesn't need much time to cook. Before roasting, for crispy outcome, you should deep fry it first, which takes only 1-2 minutes to fully cook.
FOR THE MIXTURE OF SALT
- ½ tsp: Salt
- 1tsp: Sugar

- ½ tsp: Cooking Powder
- ½ tsp: Ground Pepper
- ½ tsp: Garlic Powder

FOR ROASTING
- 10: Shrimp, deveined
- 1tsp: Cooking Wine
- 500g: Shrimp, peeled or unpeeled
- 3-4Tbsp: Vegetable Oil
- 1: Onion, cut into wedges
- ½ : Bell Pepper, cut into bite-sized pieces
- a pinch: Coriander, finely chopped
- a pinch: Spring Onions, finely chopped

To marinate the shrimp: Place shrimp in a large bowl, throw in 1tsp of Salt Mixture. Add tapioca starch or corn flour, mix well until all the shrimp is well coated. Let it rest for 10 minutes.

To deep-fry shrimp: Heat a frying pan and pour vegetable oil in. Add marinated shrimp and deep fry each side for about 1-2minutes until done. Remove from the heat immediately and transfer to a plate with kitchen towel to drain the extra oil.

To roast and salt shrimp: Retain about 1Tbsp of vegetable oil in the frying pan. Bring it back to a heat. Add onion, bell pepper and spring onion. Stir well and cook for about 1 minute. Add shrimp, stir well. Drizzle the amount of the left salt mixture to the taste in the pan. Mix well, roast for about 3-4 minutes until shrimps and vegetables are well absorbed with spices.

To assemble, remove the dish from the pan. Transfer to a deep plate. Sprinkle chopped coriander and red chili slices on top. Serve hot.

Fried Eggs With Pork

Trứng đúc thịt
Trứng = eggs; Đúc means mold or stick to; Thịt = meat (here pork meat).
In this scenario, **Trứng đúc thịt** mean eggs are cooked (fried) together with pork.
Fried Eggs with Pork is a dish that is easy to make and easy to eat. It's especially suitable for children because most of them like eating eggs, but sometimes the 'toughness' of the meat make them reluctant. With this dish, the meat is tender, delicious, and nutritious, and the freshly fried eggs attract children a lot. So it's worth a try for you if you have children.
Serve: 3-4
Preparation Time: 7-8 minutes
Cooking Time: 5 minutes
Tricks: If minced pork is stored in the fridge, you should take it out in the room temperature 10-15m minutes

before cooking so it falls apart more easily and mixes better with eggs.
- 4: Eggs
- 2tsp: Fish Sauce
- 2tsp: Cooking Powder
- ½ tsp: Pound Pepper
- 1Tbsp: Green Onion, finely chopped
- 1: Shallot, small size, finely chopped
- 140g: Pork, minced
- 1Tbsp: Vegetable Oil

In a big bowl, throw in eggs and stir well. Combine all the rest of the ingredients and add to the bowl. Mix well.

Heat a pan and add vegetable oil. Put the mixture from the bowl into the pan, and spread evenly. Let it cook for about 5 minutes on medium heat then flip to the other side. Fry for another 5 minutes until done. Fold uncovered half. Turn off the heat.

To assemble: Remove fried eggs with pork from the pan and place on a plate. Cut into any shapes you like or just simply bite-sized pieces. Serve with or without cooked rice.

Cakes

Các món bánh

Popular Street Food Cakes In Vietnam

Steamed Rice Rolled Crepes

Bánh Cuốn
Bánh = Crepe; Cuốn means Roll
This dish is made by steaming the rice flour as the batter with filled with pork and herbs then wrapping it to make the crepe. So its name has the word 'steamed'. It is very flavourful, savoury, super yummy, and it is a very popular breakfast dish in Vietnam.
Serve: 4-5
Preparation Time: 45 minutes
Cooking Time: 1 hour
Tricks: Steamed rice crepes are best when they are made one day in advance and be kept in the fridge. At

the time of serving you just need to warm them up by microwave for about 5 minutes.

FOR THE BATTER
- 1 cup: Tapioca Starch
- 1 cup: Rice Flour
- 2 cups: Warm Water
- ½ tsp: Salt
- 1Tbsp: Cooking Oil

FOR THE FILLING
- 600g: Pork, shoulder, finely chopped by hand
- a handful: Shallot, minced
- Nearly a handful: Fungus, soaked, rinsed well, minced
- 3-4: Shiitake Mushrooms, soaked, rinsed well, minced
- ½ tsp: Ground Pepper
- 1 tsp: Chicken Powder
- 1 ½ tsp: Fish Sauce
- 1Tbsp: Sugar

FOR THE DIPPING SAUCE
- 1 ½ cups: Hot Water
- 1tsp: Sugar
- 1-2: Chili Pepper, finely chopped
- 3-4 cloves: Garlic, minced

FOR THE REST
- 1: Lime, cut into 4-5 wedges, set aside for side-table condiment
- a handful: Vietnamese Balm
- a handful: Coriander

To make batter: Combine all the ingredients in a big bowl and mix well until the flour fully dissolves. Let it rest for about 30 minutes to 1 hour.

To make the filling: Combine all the ingredients in another bowl. Heat a skillet with 3Tbsp of cooking oil, add the filling mixture and sauté for about 5-8 minutes over high heat, then add sugar. Keep sautéing for about 1-2 minutes until done.

To make the dipping sauce: In the 3rd bowl, mix warm water, sugar and fish sauce until sugar fully dissolves. Add chili pepper and garlic. Top with ground pepper.

To make fried shallot: Finely slice shallots then remove the excess moisture in the sliced shallots with a paper towel. In a pan, add shallots then pour about 1 finger-breadth of cooking oil in (the oil should be enough to cover the shallots). Heat the pan over medium low heat. Fry the shallot slices slowly until they turn lightly golden. Quickly turn off the heat as the residual heat in the oil still keeps frying the shallots until they are light brown. Drain the fried shallots using a strainer. Use paper towels to drain off the excess oil. Fried shallots will become crispy when cooled.

To make the rice crepe: Spread out cling film on a flat surface like cutting board and prepare a flat surface like a large plate and grease it with ½ tsp of shallot oil. Heat 1tsp of shallot oil in a nonstick skillet over medium heat until hot. Stir up the batter then pour in about 2/3 soup ladle (small size) of the batter on the center of the skillet then slowly tilt it in a circular motion to spread out the batter evenly and create an even round crepe. Cover with the lid and keep cooking for about 30 seconds. Uncover and scoop about 1Tbsp of filling on the crepe and roll the crepe, 2 sides first then the bottom and roll up until done. Take the rolled crepe out of the skillet and transfer to a plate. Repeat the process until the batter is used up. But you do not need to regrease the skillet, as the batter has some oil already.

To assemble: Transfer the rice rolls into a serving plate, cut them into bite-sized pieces, and top with fried shallots. Serve with Vietnamese Balm and Coriander and Vietnamese Ham or Chả Lụa. Serve warm with dipping sauce and add lime juice to taste.

Steamed Rice Rolled Crepe – **Bánh Cuốn**

Fried Rice Balls

Bánh Rán

These yummy deep-fried rice balls come from the north of Vietnam. Its outer dough is made from a mixture of glutinous rice and ordinary rice flour, filled with mung bean paste and covered all over with sesame seeds. Southern Vietnam also has similar balls, called Bánh Cam, but they are often coated with sugary syrup and there's no shredded coconut in the filling.

Yield: 15 balls

Preparation Time: 1 hour

Cooking Time: 30 minutes

Tricks: The ration of flour to water should be 2 or 2.5:1. Too much or too little water will affect the result. The former will cause the balls to collapse after deep-frying, whilst the latter will cause them to explode.

You should control the oil temperature around 150oC during the deep-frying process to avoid the explosion and keep the balls a perfect golden brown color when done.

FOR THE BATTER
- 220g: Glutinous Rice Flour
- 2Tbsp: Ordinary Rice Flour
- 100ml: Luke Warm Water
- 80g: Sugar
- ¼ tsp: Salt
- 1 cup: Sesame Seeds

FOR THE FILLING
- 80g: Mung Bean, soaked,
- 3-4tsp: Sugar
- a touch: Salt
- ¼ cup: Shredded Coconut
- 1Tbsp: Cooking Oil

FOR THE REST

Cooking oil for frying

More glutinous rice flour for adjusting

In a small bowl, scoop about 2 tsp of glutinous rice flour and mix with about 1tsp of water. Knead it until smooth.

Bring a small pot with water to a boil. Add small drops of dough and cook for about 2-3 minutes. Then transfer them to a bowl of cold water cool.

To make the main dough: In a large bowl, mix the rest of glutinous flour with the rest of the ingredients for making dough. Add the small dough ball in. Knead well by hand until the mixture turns smooth. Cover and let it rest for about 30 minutes.

Divide the dough into 15 equal portions. Shape each portion into a round ball.

To make the filling: Cook mung beans in a rice cooker with about ¼ cup of water, or the water level is just enough to barely cover the beans. Then transfer mung beans to a blender and blend it into a fine paste or smash by hand using mortar and pestle or a big spoon. (Alternatively, you can use mung bean flour and turn it to paste by mixing with some water). Add sugar, shredded coconut, and vegetable oil and mix well. Divide the filling into 15 even balls.

To assemble the balls: Take one portion of dough, shape it into a bowl and then scoop about 2tsp of filling and put in the centre of the bowl. Seal it completely and shape into a round ball again. Quickly dip the ball into water and then roll it in the sesame seeds. Press the balls several times so the sesame seeds stick to the ball as much as possible. Repeat with the rest of the dough.

To fry the ball: Heat enough cooking oil to cover the balls to 150°C. You can test the temperature with a small piece of dough, if the bubbles appear around the dough so the temperature is right. Carefully place the balls and deep-fry until they are golden brown, occasionally rotate the balls so they are fried evenly. Then remove and transfer to a serving plate with a paper towel to absorb the extra oil. Serve warm or at room temperature.

Fried Rice Balls made before deep-frying – **Bánh rán**

Crispy Fried Pancake

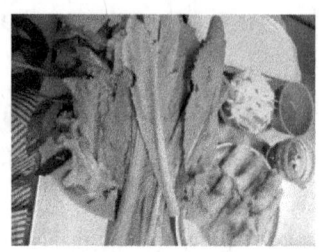

Bánh Xèo
Serve: 3-4
Preparation Time: 15 minutes
Cooking Time: 1 hour
Tricks: Make the batter a day in advance and keep in the fridge.
Do not use more tumeric powder than written in the recipe as it can make the dish acrid and the color look unnatural. The most important part of the cooking process is mixing flour which can be made in advance hours before or a day before and stored in the fridge.
Using an old frying pan helps to make the finishing cake crispier.
FOR THE BATTER
- 400g: Rice Flour
- ½ l: Coconut Milk
- ½ tsp: Salt
- ½ tsp: Chicken powder
- ½ Tbsp: Tumeric powder

FOR THE FILLING

- 200g: Shrimp, peeled, deveined
- 200g: Pork Belly, cut into thin slices
- ½ tsp: Chicken Powder
- ½ tsp: Ground Pepper
- 1Tbsp: Sugar, granulated
- 2-3 cloves: Garlic, finely chopped
- 1: Shallot, finely chopped
- a dash: Cooking Oil

FOR DIPPING SAUCE
- ½ Tbsp: Rice Vinegar
- 1Tbsp: Honey or Sugar
- ½ Tbsp: Lime
- 1Tbsp: Fish Sauce
- 5Tbsp: Water
- 2-3 cloves: Garlic, minced
- 1: Chili Pepper, finely chopped
- ¼ cup: Pickled Daikon and Carrot; **see the recipe in Grilled Pork Noodles**

FOR THE REST
- a cup: Bean Spouts
- 1: Onion, julienned
- 2Tbsp: Green Onion, finely chopped
- a cup: Mung Beans, steamed
- Mix of vegetables of your choice. There are some recommendations including mustard green, lettuce, coriander, purple basil, mint, Vietnamese balm.

To make dipping sauce: Combine all the ingredients for making dipping sauce including fish sauce, honey (or sugar), lime, and vinegar in a bowl. Mix well until the sugar or honey completely dissolves. Add pickles, minced garlic and chili pepper. Set it aside.

To make the batter: Combine all the ingredients for mixing flour in a large bowl. Stir well. Set it aside.

To marinate pork and shrimp: In another bowl, combine all the ingredients. Mix well. Set it aside.

Heat a wok or frying pan (diameter of about 20cm), pour in just a little bit vegetable oil. Use a small brush coat the whole bottom of the pan. Add pork and shrimp and cook on high heat for about 5 minutes. Ladle in enough mixing flour batter to cover the pan. Place beansprouts and cooked mung beans in the pan. Cover and let it cook for just 2 minutes until done. When pancake has cooked, fold uncovered pancake half over filling.

To assemble: Transfer the pancake to a plate. Handle a leaf of mustard green or lettuce; Place a bite-sized piece of pancake together with your favorite mix of vegetables inside this leaf and fold into a bite. Dip in dipping sauce. Serve in room temperature or warm.

www.ingramcontent.com/pod-product-compliance
Lightning Source LLC
Chambersburg PA
CBHW071441070526
44578CB00001B/184